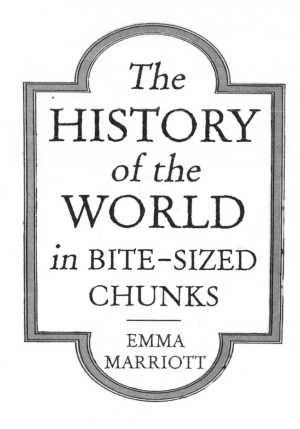

The
HISTORY
of the
WORLD
in BITE-SIZED
CHUNKS

EMMA
MARRIOTT

MJF BOOKS
NEW YORK

For my father, Charles Donald Mann (1931–2012)

Published by MJF Books
Fine Communications
322 Eighth Avenue
New York, NY 10001

The History of the World in Bite-Sized Chunks
LC Control Number: 2013930637
ISBN-13: 978-1-60671-187-3
ISBN-10: 1-60671-187-3

Designed and typeset by www.glensaville.com

This edition is published by MJF Books in arrangement with
Michael O'Mara Books Limited.

Printed in the United States of America.

MJF Books and the MJF colophon are trademarks of Fine Creative Media, Inc.

QF   10   9   8   7   6   5   4   3   2

CONTENTS

LIST OF MAPS

INTRODUCTION

Our aim with this book was to encapsulate nearly 5,000 years of world history in one, relatively slim volume. The vast and often complex nature of our global history was to be distilled down into a format both simple and accessible, into a collection of 'bite-sized chunks'.

Added to this, we resolved to give due prominence to the world's earliest civilizations and ancient empires, and to provide a history of the world that would also venture beyond the well-trodden paths of European history.

The familiar stories of European and North American history are of course here, from the glories of the Ancient Greeks and the Norman invasions to the American Wars of Independence and the Wall Street Crash. But we also delve into the events and peoples of the Far East, Africa, the Middle East, Oceania and the Americas, to highlight, albeit briefly (as is the nature of the book), such gems as the Indus civilization in Pakistan, the Tang dynasty in China, the Kush kingdom in North Africa, and Nadir Shah in Persia.

Each entry is concise but comprehensive, a self-contained morsel of information that can be consumed on its own or digested alongside its fellow entries. We've tried to cover as much as we can within one volume (although it's often more difficult to decide what should be left out than what should stay in). Cross-references are also given in the text to other entries and events, as history is nothing if not interlinked and shaped by what has gone before.

We begin with the world's earliest civilizations, of which

we know relatively little, but which nonetheless have great influence on life today. (In the words of the historian J. M. Roberts: 'Distant history still clutters up our lives, and our thinking.') Thereafter more than fifty-four centuries of world history are covered right up to 1945, with the entries split into subgroups encompassing the Middle East and Africa, Europe, the Americas, the Far East and Oceania. Often, modern names of countries and cities have been given, although older names have been retained when deemed more appropriate and familiar to the reader.

Our hope is that *The History of the World in Bite-Sized Chunks* will have pruned away some of the confusing mesh of history in order to get to some of its key facts, from mass migration and conflict to the dazzling achievements of the past and the numerous examples of man's tenacity to survive, all of which still influences our thinking and makes us what we are today.

EMMA MARRIOTT

Grateful thanks to Dr Hilary Stroh (née Larkin), Lindsay Davies, David Woodroffe, Ana Bježančević, Greg Stevenson, Andrew John, Charlotte Buchan, Dominique Enright and Glen Saville.

CHAPTER ONE:
FIRST EMPIRES AND CIVILIZATIONS

3500 BC to 800 BC

MIDDLE EAST AND AFRICA

SUMERIA

In about 5000 BC, farmers settled on the fertile land of southern Mesopotamia (now Iraq) known as Sumer, and from these humble beginnings the world's first great civilization formed. Living along the river valleys of the Tigris and Euphrates (Mesopotamia is Greek for the land 'between two rivers'), Sumerian farmers were able to grow an abundance of grain and other crops, the surplus of which enabled them to settle in one place. Sumerians also traded this surplus food for metals and tools with people as far away as present-day Pakistan and Afghanistan, and they dug a network of ditches and canals as drainage channels on their fertile but flood-prone lands.

By 3000 BC, a number of city-states had developed in Sumer, the largest being Ur, with a population of 40,000. The first known system of writing originated in Sumer: at first pictographic, it gradually evolved into a series of simplified wedge-shaped signs formed using reed stalks on clay tablets (the script came to be called 'cuneiform', meaning 'wedge-shaped' in Latin). Sumerians also devised complex administrative and legal systems, developed wheeled vehicles and potters' wheels, and built great ziggurats and buildings with columns and domes.

The first great empire of Sumer was established by Sargon, king of Akkad (an ancient kingdom situated north of Sumer), in about 2350 BC. All Sumerian cities were united under his control and the empire stretched from Syria to the Persian Gulf. This dynasty was destroyed in about 2200 BC but after 2150 BC the kings of Ur re-established Sumerian authority in Sumer and also conquered Akkad. Following an invasion by the Elamites (a civilization to the east of Sumer) and the sack of Ur in around 2000 BC, Sumer came under Amorite rule, out of which emerged the great city-state of Babylon (see page 14).

ANCIENT EGYPT: THE OLD KINGDOM

The first great civilization in Africa began with the settlement of the Nile valley in the north-east of the continent in around 5000 BC. It's now thought these early settlers were from the Sahara, where, some 2,000 years earlier, Africa's first farming societies had developed before climate change had turned the Sahara into desert. This same climate change had dried out the swamps of the Nile valley, making it more of an attractive settlement for farming people.

By the mid-fourth millenium BC, the valley of the Nile was densely populated, towns had grown and the region had been divided into two Egyptian kingdoms. Traditional Egyptian chronology tells us that in 3200 BC, the pharaoh (ruler)

Menes unified the two kingdoms of Egypt to create a single state. This saw the beginning of a 3,000-year civilization that was marked by monumental tomb-building projects and a flourishing of Egyptian culture.

The earliest period of Ancient Egypt, known as the Old Kingdom (*c.* 2575–2130 BC), was ruled by a number of powerful pharaohs and saw major developments in technology, art and architecture. During this era, hieroglyphic script was developed and the Great Sphinx and Giza pyramids were constructed (during which thousands of ordinary Egyptians died). The pyramids provided for the after-life of the pharaoh, and were closely associated with the cult of the sun-god Ra – their flared shape resembled the rays of the sun and provided for the deceased king a stairway to the gods.

ANCIENT EGYPT: THE MIDDLE AND NEW KINGDOMS

A period of stability in Egypt, known as the Middle Kingdom (*c.* 1938–1630 BC), followed a century of severe drought, famine and the collapse of central government.

Thereafter, Egypt's pharaohs restored the country's prosperity and stability, by securing its borders, increasing its agricultural output and acquiring vast mineral wealth (partly by reconquering land in lower Nubia that was rich in quarries and gold mines). This era was known for its jewellery and goldsmiths' designs. The worship of Osiris, god of death and rebirth, also spread across Egypt, leading to the prevailing belief that everyone, not just the pharaohs, would be welcomed by the gods after death.

Ambitious building and mineral projects, along with severe floods along the Nile, led to a weakening of the pharaoh's power in Egypt, enabling foreign settlers (mainly Hyksos, who were probably from Palestine) to seize control. The shift from a bronze- to an iron-based economy also contributed to the decline. This was followed by the New Kingdom (*c.* 1539–1075 BC), when control was re-established by the pharaohs and Egyptian influence extended into Syria, Nubia and the Middle East. Regarded as one of the greatest chapters of Egyptian history, many great temples were built, including the painted tombs of the Valley of the Kings. The era also included the reign of some of Egypt's most famous pharaohs, including the female ruler Hatshepsut and the boy-king Tutankhamun.

Following the death of Egypt's last great pharaoh, Rameses III, in 1070 BC, Egypt went into slow decline as it split into several small kingdoms. In around 719 BC, the Kushites (see page 34) conquered Egypt and ruled as pharaohs until they were pushed back to their own borders by Assyrians in 656 BC. Assyrian rule was followed by Persian conquest in 525 BC, occupation by Alexander the Great in 332 BC and finally Roman conquest in 30 BC.

BABYLONIA

Political power in Mesopotamia eventually moved north to the city of Babylon in Akkad, so that the entire plain became known as Babylonia. The first great dynasty of Babylon lasted about 300 years from around 1894 BC, reaching the peak of its influence under King Hammurabi (*c.* 1795–1750 BC).

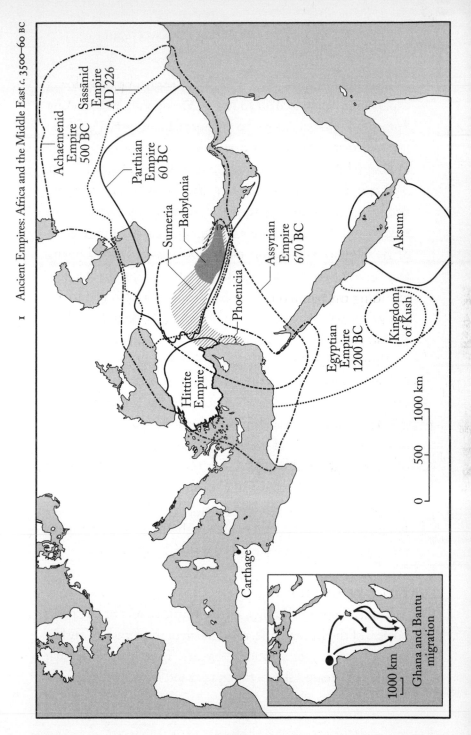

1   Ancient Empires: Africa and the Middle East *c.* 3500–60 BC

During Hammurabi's rule, the empire of Babylonia expanded to include all of southern Mesopotamia (including Sumer) and part of Assyria to the north. Hammurabi is famed for instituting the world's first known set of laws (the code of Hammurabi) and also promoting science and scholarship.

After Hammurabi's death, the Babylonian Empire declined, and from 1595 BC was dominated by Hittites (see below) and then by Kassites (mountain people from the east of Babylonia) who established a 400-year dynasty. During this time Assyria broke away from Babylonia, and a struggle ensued over several centuries for the control of Babylon. By the ninth century BC, Assyrian kings ruled Babylonia until the fall of the Assyrian Empire in the late seventh century BC.

Thereon, Babylonia fell under the power of the Chaldeans (a little-known Semitic people) and the empire prospered again, most notably under Nebuchadrezzar II (604–562 BC). He conquered Assyria and Palestine and revitalized the city of Babylon, rebuilding the temple of Marduk (the main god of Babylonia) and constructing the celebrated 'Hanging Gardens'. In 539 BC Babylon was invaded by the Persians, under Cyrus the Great (see page 28), and the Babylonian Empire came to an end – although the city of Babylon remained important well into the fourth century BC.

Hittite Empire

The warrior people known as the Hittites, one of the great powers of the Bronze Age, ruled much of modern-day Turkey and Syria for over a thousand years. Their empire, which reached its greatest size between 1450 and 1200 BC, rivalled the empires of Babylonia and Assyria, as well as Ancient Egypt.

Much of what we know about the Hittites stems from the discovery of 10,000 cuneiform clay tablets in Hattusas, Turkey, in 1906. These, along with the remains of some of their ancient cities, revealed that the Hittites were feudal tribesmen who, not long after 3000 BC, swept south from a region north of the Black Sea into Anatolia, or Asia Minor, which is today the Asian part of Turkey. They rode horses and chariots, and were equipped with bronze daggers. By 2000 BC, Hittite dominions were united into an empire, with its capital at Hattusas. One of the first Hittite kings, Hattusili I (1650–1620 BC), invaded Syria, and his successor, Mursili I, sacked Babylon, although he was later killed and Hittite conquests were lost.

A still more powerful Hittite Empire arose in 1450 BC and by c. 1380 BC the great Hittite king Suppiluliumas had built an empire that encompassed Syria almost to Canaan (modern-day Israel). By the time of his descendant Muwatallis, Egypt and the Hittite Empire competed over dominance in Syria, which led to a fierce and much famed battle between the Egyptian pharaoh Rameses II and Muwatallis at Qadesh (c. 1300 BC).

It's thought that the Hittites were the first civilization to produce iron on a large scale, using it for tools and weaponry, thus initiating the Iron Age (although iron wasn't used by most civilizations until several centuries later). Hittite power suddenly collapsed when migrants, including Aegean Sea people (a mysterious coalition of migrants from the eastern Mediterranean), invaded the region c. 1193 BC.

ASSYRIA

In the fourteenth century BC, Assyria broke away from Babylonia (see pages 14–16) and established an independent empire originally centred on the city of Assur in northern Mesopotamia.

Constant warfare with invaders from the north and south turned the Assyrians into fierce fighters, much famed for their cruelty. With a language almost identical to the Babylonians (whose culture the Assyrians has absorbed), the Assyrians were innovative in their weapon technology, developing the use of siege engines. It is also believed that they were the first to use horses as cavalry, rather than as chariot bearers.

The most famous of Assyrian kings, Sargon II (722–705 BC), moved the capital to Nineveh and conquered, amongst other places, Damascus and Israel, exiling 30,000 Israelites (the basis behind the legend of the Ten Lost Tribes of Israel).

By the seventh century BC, Assyria had become the largest empire the world had ever seen, and the last of the great Assyrian kings, Ashurbanipal (668–627 BC), ruled over an empire that stretched from the Persian Gulf up to and including Egypt. To govern such an empire, the Assyrians built roads and organized a highly effective mail service, whilst Ashurbanipal created and constructed in Nineveh the Middle East's first organized library, which contained thousands of text and clay tablets. Some 20,720 of these cuneiform tablets are now housed in the British Museum.

The Assyrian state was finally defeated in 612 BC by a coalition of Medes (Indo-European people related to the Persians) and Chaldeans. Over the following centuries,

Assyria was ruled by Babylon, the Persian Empire, Alexander the Great (who renamed it Syria), the Parthians, and the Romans.

PHOENICIA

By 2000 BC, many people had settled on the coast of the eastern Mediterranean in modern-day Lebanon, Syria and Israel. Living on a narrow, coastal strip that formed the natural communication point between Asia, Africa and beyond, these settlers grew and produced various commodities, including cedar wood (used for building), olives, wine and cloth, which they traded with Egypt, Cyprus, Crete and places as far away as Troy in western Turkey.

By 1500 BC, new cities had begun to be built in the region to add to the cities of Ugarit and Byblos, which had been founded as early as 4000 and 3000 BC respectively. Set against the decline of parallel empires, Phoenician cities – the greatest being Tyre, Sidon and Berot, all famed for their embroideries – had entered into a golden age by 1000 BC.

Trade continued to form the cornerstone of Phoenician prosperity, in particular the manufacture and trade of luxury items such as gold and silver ornaments, fine glassware and carved ivory. Phoenician dyes and – most notably – its famous purple textiles became much sought after (purple fabrics were increasingly associated with superior social status). Indeed the name Phoenicia is derived from the Greek word for 'purple'.

Becoming a maritime power, the Phoenicians began to establish colonies in Cyprus and all along the North African coast from the end of the ninth century BC, and in

814 BC they established Carthage in Tunisia (see pages 35–6). Phoenicia still thrived under the control of the Assyrian and then Persian Empires until 322 BC, when its capital Tyre was sacked and it was incorporated into the Greek world of Alexander the Great.

FAR EAST

INDUS CIVILIZATION

One of the most highly developed urban communities in the world emerged in the lower valley of the River Indus, in modern-day Pakistan, in *c.* 2500 BC. More advanced in many ways than Ancient Egypt, it was certainly bigger, covering an area of over 190,000 square miles (500,000 square km), compared to Egypt's 24,000 square miles (63,000 square km). It is also the earliest south-Asian civilization, owing its growth to the fertility of the Indus valley.

To date, some 100 sites relating to the Indus civilization have been unearthed by archaeologists and excavations are still being carried out. The largest of these settlements include the cities of Harappa, Mohenjo-daro and Dholavira, which each had a population of around 30–40,000. Substantial buildings made of baked brick, set within a grid pattern of streets, testify to careful urban planning and uniformity throughout many of the cities and towns of the Indus valley. Indus settlements were also marked by some of the most advanced plumbing and drainage systems in the world – almost every domestic compound in Mohenjo-daro was provided with a toilet in the form of a brick culvert, connected to brick-lined sewers running under the streets.

Indus script, formed of around 400 different signs and found largely on soapstone stamp seals, has yet to be deciphered, so that many important questions about the Indus civilization still remain unanswered. Weaponry has not as yet been found, nor evidence of organized religion, and there is still no definitive explanation for the sudden collapse of the Indus civilization in around 1500 BC. It may have been caused by flooding, overpopulation, or a build-up of salt in the soil, or its cities may have been destroyed by Aryan invaders (see below).

THE VEDIC AGE AND HINDUISM

The Vedic Age (*c.* 1500–800 BC) relates to a period in history when the ancient Hindu scriptures know as the Vedas were composed. Made up of four sacred books, they are regarded as the historical predecessor of Hinduism. The Vedic Age is also associated with the arrival of Aryan invaders into India at around 1500 BC. These were noble nomadic people from central Asia – the word 'Aryan' originally meant 'noble'.

There are no true historical accounts of the Aryan migrations, but they are referred to in the *Rigveda* texts, the oldest of the Vedas scriptures, as tribespeople whose lives revolved around their horses and herds of cattle. The Aryans spoke an early form of Sanskrit, the language of the Hindu scriptures, which in the vernacular evolved into several modern languages including Hindi, the official language of modern India.

In the centuries following the arrival of the Aryans,

northern India was gradually aryanized. The pale-coloured Aryans initially refused to intermingle with the dark-skinned inhabitants of India and a rigid social hierarchy developed, made up of four divisions: the Brahmin (priests or scholars), Kshatriyas (soldiers), Vaishyas (farmers or merchants) and Shudras (servants). These formed the basis of the Hindu caste system.

The Vedic forms of belief are seen as the precursor to modern Hinduism. Its main deities included Indra, Agni (the sacrificial fire) and Suyra (the sun). Some of the classical Hindu gods, like Vishnu, held only minor significance, whilst others, like Shiva, were absent altogether. The performance of sacrifices was central to Vedic worship, especially the offering of Soma (a hallucinogenic drink) to the gods. By the later Vedic period, the religion of the conquered people in India had combined with the traditions of the Vedas to form early Hinduism.

EARLY CHINESE CIVILIZATION

In China, the earliest form of civilization to emerge is known as the Xia dynasty. Scant archaeological findings have led to disagreement over whether the Xia civilization actually existed, but it is thought that it may have appeared in around 2100 BC, in the Yellow River valley, where archaeologists have found stone tools and a bronze smelter dating from 2000 BC.

The subsequent Shang dynasty, which was based near modern Anyang from 1766 BC, is better understood, largely as a result of the discovery of inscriptions on more than 100,000 tortoise shells. Shang people tried to predict the future by heating the bones or shells of animals (known as orack bones), and the inscriptions relating to this are the earliest known records of Chinese writing. By about 1500 BC the Shang dynasty was flourishing and advances included the casting of bronze for sacred vessels and weapons, the development of a sophisticated writing system, and the intricate carving of jade and ivory. The size and extent of the Shang kingdom is uncertain, but it's likely it extended over some 402,000 miles (647,500 km).

In about 1046 BC, the rulers of the Zhou kingdom took over from the Shang rulers, to form a dynasty that survived for nearly 800 years (the most long-lived in Chinese history). The dynasty ruled territory to the north of the Yangtze River, and in 771 BC their capital moved from Hao to Luoyang. Thereon, fighting between kingdoms and feudal lords kept China divided (a feudal system had been imposed in China well over a thousand years before the same social system evolved in Europe). During the Zhou dynasty, multiplication tables were developed and advances were made in iron casting and agricultural production. The Five Classics of Confucianism were also compiled during this time, and studied thereafter by centuries of Chinese scholars.

EUROPE

Minoan Civilization

The Minoan civilization, which appeared on the island of Crete between 3000 and 1450 BC, was the first civilization to emerge in Europe (and also one of the first to develop in an area that wasn't the flood plain of a river). The Minoans left behind great palaces, fine pottery and metalwork in gold and bronze, while Greek legend remembers Minoa as a lost and golden land.

On their mountainous island, the Minoans intensively farmed olives, wheat and vines, kept sheep on their mountain pastures, and fished. The resulting produce was exported as far away as Egypt, Syria and Cyprus. By 2000 BC, the wealth generated from this extensive trade led to the development of cities and ports, dominated by the magnificent palaces of Knossos, Mallia, Phaistos and Zākros. The biggest of these, Knossos, was discovered in 1900 by the English archaeologist Arthur Evans (prior to which nothing was known about Minoan civilization).

The Minoans feature in a number of Greek legends, including the Cretan half-man, half-bull monster, the Minotaur (the bull was a sacred animal to the Minoans). The Minoans also developed an as-yet undeciphered script based on syllabic symbols, known as Linear A.

Around 1700 BC, most of the Minoan palaces were destroyed by fire, either as a result of war or earthquake, and then rebuilt, with the Minoans subsequently producing pottery and frescoes of the highest quality. In around 1500 BC a huge volcanic eruption on the island of Thera (now Santorini) generated a tidal wave that again damaged Minoan palaces and towns, destroying most of their ships, though they were soon repaired and Crete remained prosperous for several years after the eruption. The Minoan civilization came to end c. 1450 BC as the Mycenaeans (see below) took control of the Aegean.

Mycenaean Civilization

The Mycenaean were a prosperous, artistic and warlike people who lived on mainland Greece, on the plain of Argos. An Aegean civilization like the Minoans, their period of greatness began in *c.* 1600 BC, when they began to build a number of small, fortified cities, most notably the settlements of Tiryns, Pylos and Mycenae. Most cities were built on natural strongholds, with palaces to house their ruling kings, surrounded by strong, defensive walls.

In 1450 BC, the Mycenaean occupied Crete and took over the Minoan sea trade, sailing to Asia Minor and Syria and trading with Sicily and Italy. They also began the process of Greek colonization (which reached its greatest extent during the period of Classical Greece) by setting up colonies in Rhodes, Cyprus and on the south-west coast of Anatolia.

The Mycenaean also converted Minoan script into a form of Greek, which has been translated to reveal that the Mycenaean worshipped several of the Classical Greek gods including Poseidon, Apollo and Zeus. Warfare featured prominently in Mycenaean art, which also borrowed much from Minoan culture – but remained distinct – with the production of bronze vessels, armour and weaponry, and gold masks. The Mycenaean are also famous for their shaft graves and tombs.

In 1200 BC, according to legend, the Mycenaeans sacked Troy (which lay on the Mediterranean coast of Anatolia) although the scale of the expedition was probably vastly exaggerated in Homer's depiction in the *Iliad*. Mycenaean civilization collapsed in around 1120 BC: it's generally unknown what led to this, although it occurred at a time of general turmoil in the eastern Mediterranean (the Hittite Empire collapsed abruptly in 1205 BC) and may have had something to do with the invasions of the Aegean Sea Peoples.

THE AMERICAS

OLMEC AND CHAVÍN CIVILIZATIONS

The first recognized civilization to emerge in the Americas occurred in the swampy Veracruz lowlands of the eastern Mexican coast and Gulf Coast. Farming, villages and pottery had appeared in Central America since the second millennium BC, out of which grew the Olmec civilization in around 1500 BC.

The focus point for the Olmecs seems to have been large ceremonial sites where earth pyramids have been found alongside giant sculpted stone heads, which are thought to commemorate their rulers. These ceremonial sites had populations of thousands. One of the largest was at La Venta, which flourished until 400 BC and which supported a prosperous community of farmers, fishers, traders and artisans. For several centuries after 800 BC, the characteristic style of Olmec art (which often fused human infant and jaguar-like figures) spread right across central America to modern day El Salvador.

Olmec culture disappeared at around 400 BC, as newer civilizations, such as the Maya (see pages 70–2), overtook it. Mystery still surrounds the Olmecs, as it's not known what language they spoke or what exactly led to their demise.

Much further south, in Peru, the Chavín civilization, which was centred on the ceremonial site of Chavín de Huantar located high up in the Andes, flourished from around 900 BC to 200 BC. The Chavín people also had a high level of skill in stone working and an artistic style that spread to much of the Andes region. Two hundred finely worked stone sculptures were discovered at Chavín de Huántar, and this may have been a pilgrimage site for people across Peru.

CHAPTER TWO:
THE ANCIENT WORLD

800 BC to AD 450

MIDDLE EAST AND AFRICA

THE ACHAEMENIAN EMPIRE

In 559 BC, a young king named Cyrus II (the Great) came to power in Persia and over the next decade built an empire that would eventually rule over a fifth of the world's population. The Persian dynasty of kings was called the Achaemenid, after the Iranian king, Achaemenes.

In around 549 BC, Cyrus mobilized his people and conquered the Medes (Indo-Europeans living in northern Iran who had control of Persia), acquiring Assyria in the process. Two years later, Cyrus's formidable armies controlled Ionian Greek cities, and in 539 BC captured Babylon, along with Palestine, to which he allowed the exiled Jews to return and rebuild their temple in Jerusalem. Just before he died in 529 BC, he expanded the empire to the borders of India.

By the time of Darius I (522–486 BC), the empire's borders encompassed Egypt, and stretched from northern India in the east to Turkey in the west, equating to the largest empire the world had seen. To help keep control of this vast domain, King Darius I introduced an effective system of administration and taxes, and built in 500 BC a 1,500 mile (2,400 km) road from Susa in modern Iran to Ephesus in Turkey.

It was around this time that the ancient Persian religion of Zoroastrianism became more established. Originally developing from Iran *c.* 600 BC, its concepts of resurrection, the final judgment, and heaven and hell would also influence the world religions of Islam, Judaism and Christianity.

From 500 BC the Ionian Greek settlements rebelled, and in 490 BC Darius sent an army to Athens to punish them for aiding the rebels. He suppressed them but was later beaten in the famous Battle of Marathon, which sparked the Persian Wars between Greece and Persia. Darius's successor, Xerxes, attempted to take control of Greece, burning Athens in 480 BC, but he was ultimately defeated later in the same year. This marked the beginning of Persia's decline, until the empire was eventually conquered in 330 by Alexander the Great.

THE PARTHIAN EMPIRE

After a period of Macedonian and Greek rule (known as the Seleucid Empire), Iran in 247 BC came under the control of Parthia, a small kingdom in north-east Persia. Over the next few centuries, the Parthians built up an empire (also known as the Arsacid dynasty) that at its height stretched from the northern reaches of the Euphrates to the Indus. Situated also on the Silk Road trade route (see pages 46, 56, 87, 90) between China and the Roman Empire, the Parthian Empire became a hub of trade and commerce.

Among notable Parthian rulers were Mithridates I

(*c.* 171–138 BC), who modelled himself on the great Persian ruler, Darius I, and the powerful kings, Mithridates II (*c.* 123–88 BC) and Phraates III (*c.* 70–57 BC). The Parthians had considerable skills in warfare and horsemanship – Parthian archers were able to shoot behind them as they rode (known as the 'Parthian shot') which gave them a huge advantage in battle.

The Parthian Empire adopted a mix of Persian, Greek and regional cultures, although the Arsacid court, which had retained some of its Greek influence, gradually saw a revival of Iranian traditions. As Parthia expanded westward, it eventually came into conflict with Rome, initially over the control of Armenia. The Parthians resoundingly defeated Marcus Licinius Crassus at the Battle of Carrhae in 53 BC (one of the worst military disasters in Roman history, in which a Roman army of 44,000 soldiers were routed, with only 10,000 men escaping alive). This battle effectively finished off Roman ambitions in the East. In the ensuing Roman–Parthian wars (66 BC–AD 217), several Roman emperors invaded the region, at one point seizing the Parthian capital of Ctesiphon. In the end, however, instability and war among Parthian's own rulers led to the collapse of Parthian power when Ardashīr I, a ruler from the Fars province of Iran, established the Sāssānid dynasty in AD 224 (see below).

THE SĀSSĀNID EMPIRE

The Sāssānid Empire, established by Ardashīr I in AD 224, is considered to be one of the most important and influential periods in Iranian history, when ancient Persian culture (prior to the Muslim conquests) reached its peak.

The Sāssānid court at the city of Ctesiphon became a focus for brilliant culture, where scholars studied astronomy, arts, medicine and philosophy and engaged in such pastimes as chess and polo. Sāssānid artwork strongly influenced Islamic art and its impact was also felt further afield in China, central Asia and even Western Europe. The Sāssānid are also famous for their rock sculptures.

The establishment of the empire, which stretched from the Syrian desert to north-west India, led to almost constant warfare, principally with Rome, as well as with the Huns, Turks and the Byzantine Empire. During the conquest of Armenia, King Shāpūr I (AD 240/42–272) is famed for his defeat and imprisonment of the Roman emperor Valerian at the Battle of Edessa in AD 260. In AD 296 the Romans regained the upper hand and the Sāssānid were subsequently driven out from Armenia and Mesopotamia. Politically, the empire fluctuated between strong monarchs (like Khosrau I who died in AD 579) and local control by great nobles. The empire disintegrated in the seventh century, prior to the Arab conquests, and Zoroastrianism declined accordingly.

THE HEBREWS AND THEIR 'ONE TRUE GOD'

The Hebrews were Semitic nomads who had migrated to Canaan from the east in the late second millennium BC. Following the defeat of the Philistines ('Sea People' invaders who had settled on the coast of Palestine), King David (1006–962 BC), with the help of the Phoenician King Hiram of Tyre, had formed a unified Palestine, with Jerusalem as its religious and political capital. After 930 BC, however, the country was again split: Israel in the north; and Judea, including Jerusalem, in the south.

In 721 BC Assyria took control of Israel and by 586 BC Judea fell under Babylonian rule, during which time Jerusalem was destroyed. The Judeans (now known as Jews, as distinct from Hebrews and Israelites), who were held captive in Babylon, began to write down their history in what would become the Jewish Torah and the first books of the Christian Bible. In 538 BC, as Babylon fell to the Persians, the Jews were allowed to return to Jerusalem, where the religious and political foundations of Judaism were laid. Some Jews decided to stay in Babylon, thus forming the first of the Jewish diaspora.

By this time, the Jews had developed a strong sense of themselves as the chosen people of a single, all-powerful God, the 'one true God' that, according to religious scriptures, had appeared to the herdsman Abraham in the early half of the second millennium BC. This worship of one god, known as monotheism, would influence the religions of Christianity and Islam, which also shared the spiritual forebear of Abraham (in the Bible, Jesus is a descendant of Abraham, and in Muslim tradition, Abraham is the 'Father of the Prophets' and ancestor of Arabic and Jewish people).

In 333 BC Alexander the Great conquered Palestine, and thereon the region fell under the control of a number of rulers, to include the Roman, Sāssānid and Byzantine empires. The Jewish presence dwindled and Galilee became its main religious centre. In AD 636 the Arabs conquered the region and Palestine remained under Muslim control for another 1,300 years.

The Birth of Christianity

In around AD 30, a Jewish carpenter named Jesus who lived in Galilee in Jewish Palestine (by now a Roman province) began preaching to fellow Jews of the one God to whom all would answer. His teachings proved popular and he soon acquired many followers (twelve of whom, known as the apostles, he selected to teach his message). Jesus spoke of a compassionate and merciful God, a god for all men of all races, for whom the principles of charity, humility and sincerity overrode those of ceremonial observances.

His teachings soon brought him into conflict with the Jewish authorities, who regarded him as a political and social subversive. In Jerusalem, he was condemned to death by the Sanhedrin, the highest Jewish court, who then brought him before the Roman governor, Pontius Pilate, who ordered his death by crucifixion. Three days after his crucifixion, his followers claimed he rose from the dead, which justified their belief that he was the Messiah or Christ ('Anointed One' in Greek).

Over the next two centuries, the teachings of Jesus, as enshrined in the four gospels of the New Testament, spread around the Roman world. The process was aided in part by the writings of a former tent maker from Asia Minor, later known as St Paul, who wrote thirteen of the twenty-seven books of the New Testament. Roman emperors tried in vain to stamp out the spread of this dangerous new cult with widespread persecutions, most intensely under Decius in AD 250 and Diocletian in AD 303–11. Finally, in AD 313 the emperor Constantine issued an edict of toleration, and from

AD 324 he began the process of making Christianity the official religion of the Roman Empire (completed in AD 381 at the Council of Constantinople). Thereafter, Christianity spread throughout Europe and beyond, becoming a major influence in the shaping of Western civilization.

THE KINGDOM OF KUSH

The kingdom of Kush – the first important African state other than Egypt – was based in the upper regions of Nubia (now Sudan) and grew to such strength that it conquered Ancient Egypt for just over a hundred years.

From around 2000 BC, the kingdom was largely dominated by its northern neighbour of Egypt, although the Kushites had developed a rich and individual culture. However, in around 1000 BC, as Egypt's influence weakened, Kushite rulers gained nominal independence and by 800 BC a new Kush kingdom was established with a capital at Napata. By about 715 BC, the Kushites, under the leadership of King Piye and King Shabaka, had overthrown the Egyptian ruling dynasty and conquered all of Egypt. The Kushites ruled as pharaohs until about 654 BC, possibly from their new capital at Memphis, when an Assyrian invasion forced them to retreat back to Kush.

The Kushite civilization continued to thrive, however, and in around 591 BC its capital moved southwards to the city of Meroë. Located on the east bank of the Nile and close to the Red Sea, trade flourished in the capital – particularly in locally produced luxury goods made of ebony, gold and ivory – and Meroë grew into a major city with temples, houses

and palaces. Meroë also had rich supplies of iron ore and timber, which provided the fuel for one of Africa's first iron industries. The Kushites were also one of the earliest people to develop an alphabetic script (as yet untranslated).

By the third century AD, the Kushite civilization was in decline, probably due to the exhaustion of local natural resources, and the loss of Red Sea trade to the neighbouring kingdom of Aksum (which in AD 350 eventually invaded Kush and destroyed Meroë).

CARTHAGINIAN ERA

The city of Carthage, situated on the coastline of modern-day Tunisia and founded by the Phoenicians (see page 19) in 814 BC, quickly expanded into one of the largest cities on the North African coast. Its foundation also forms the basis of various legends, in particular the *Aeneid* by the Roman poet Virgil, in which Queen Dido, having fled the Phoenician city of Tyre, founds Carthage.

In around 600 BC, Carthage broke away from Phoenician control, and further established itself as a major trading centre, linking the African interior with the Mediterranean world. Its wealth was based on seafaring and trade, along with the excavation of silver mines in North Africa and southern Spain.

Carthage's interests in North Africa, Spain and Sicily (where it established colonies) eventually brought it into conflict, first with Greece in the fifth century BC and then with Rome in the Punic Wars beginning in 264 BC. The second Punic War (218–201 BC) was fought by the commander of Spain, Hannibal, who famously took an army of men and forty elephants across the Alps towards Rome. His greatest victory was at Cannae in 216 BC where 60,000 Roman soldiers were killed.

Hannibal, however, ultimately failed to defeat Rome, and by the end of the third Punic War (146 BC), Carthage was destroyed by the Romans, with some 200,000 inhabitants massacred and the remaining 50,000 sold into slavery. Carthage was then re-founded as a Roman city, during which time it prospered, later becoming a centre of Christianity. In AD 533 it was incorporated into the Byzantine Empire, and was eventually destroyed by the Arabs in AD 705, and replaced by Tunis.

FAR EAST

BUDDHISM

The Buddhist faith stems from the teachings of Siddarth Gautama who was born in around 563 BC in northern India. Gautama came from a wealthy background, but at the age of twenty-nine he decided to give up his riches and live as a beggar so that he could search for the true meaning of life. In around 528 BC, he sat beneath a bodhi tree and found enlightenment, and thereon dedicated the rest of his life to teaching others what he had learnt.

The central theme of his teachings (the Dhamma) and the faith of Buddhism is that all phenomena are linked together by a central chain of dependency; that the world's suffering is caused by selfish desire; and that only by following the

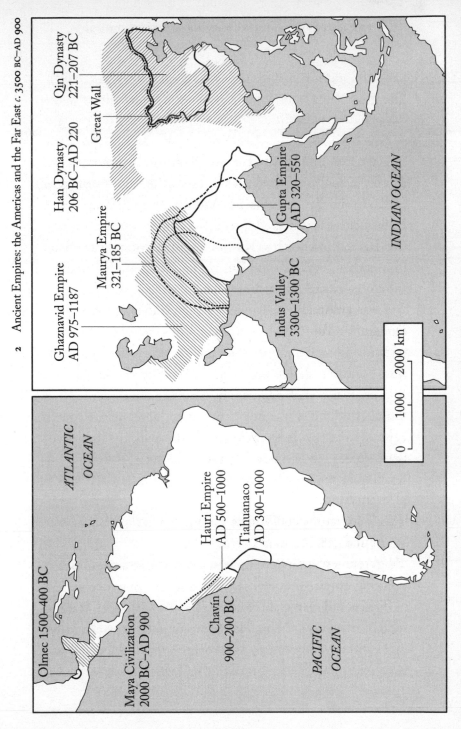

2 Ancient Empires: the Americas and the Far East *c.* 3500 BC–AD 900

Ghaznavid Empire
AD 975–1187

Maurya Empire
321–185 BC

Han Dynasty
206 BC–AD 220

Qin Dynasty
221–207 BC

Great Wall

Gupta Empire
AD 320–550

Indus Valley
3300–1300 BC

INDIAN OCEAN

0   1000   2000 km

ATLANTIC
OCEAN

Olmec 1500–400 BC

Maya Civilization
2000 BC–AD 900

Hauri Empire
AD 500–1000

Tiahuanaco
AD 300–1000

Chavin
900–200 BC

PACIFIC
OCEAN

path of Buddha can one be released from the cycle of rebirth. The goal of life is to reach a state of 'nirvana', literally the 'blowing out of desire'.

Siddarth Gautama became known as Buddha ('the enlightened one') and after his death in around 482 BC, monks helped spread his teachings throughout northern India. In the third century BC, Ashoka, Maurya Emperor of India (see below), helped spread Buddhism south to Ceylon (Sri Lanka) and north to Kashmir, sent missionaries to Syan (Siam, now Thailand) and Burma, and built many Buddhist monuments and monasteries.

From around AD 150, trade between India, China and the Roman Empire led to Mahayana monks taking the teaching of Buddha to China. In the third century, key Buddhist texts were translated into Chinese, and by the fourth and fifth centuries AD, Buddhism became the dominant faith in China. Buddhism was first brought to Korea in the fourth century, and was later introduced to Japan at some point between AD 550 and 600. At the same time, it declined in India to be replaced by Hinduism.

THE MAURYA AND GUPTA EMPIRE AND THE GOLDEN AGE OF INDIA

The Maurya Empire (*c.* 321–185 BC) was a large and politically powerful empire in India. The first example of a state system in the subcontinent, it was founded by Chandragupta Maurya, who overthrew the Nanda kingdom in north-eastern India, and in 305 BC took control of provinces in Afghanistan and much of modern-day Pakistan following a victory over

Alexander the Great's former general, Seleukos.

Maurya's son gained control over most of southern India and his grandson, Ashoka, secured a small kingdom, Kalinga, and devoted much of his rule to promoting Buddhism (see page 36). After Ashoka's death in 232 BC, the empire splintered into several small kingdoms, to include Greek principalities in the Punjab from 170 BC, and in AD 50 the Kushana Empire in northern India, which eventually became a dependency of the Sāssānid Empire (see page 30) in AD 240.

In AD 320 Chandragupta I, ruler of the Magadha kingdom, enlarged his empire, and under subsequent Gupta kings, the empire extended to include most of India. The Gupta dynasty is often called the 'Golden Age of India', as art, architecture and literature flourished during long periods of peace and prosperity. Wonderful palaces and temples were built and major literature written in Sanskrit, including the epic stories of the Mahrabharata and the Ramayana, crucial to the development of Hinduism, which are still retold and re-enacted across south-east Asia today. The Guptas are probably also responsible for the development of Brahmanism as a theological concept.

In addition – and often wrongly attributed to the Arabs who simply passed it on to the Europeans – the Guptas invented the so-called 'Arabic' method of writing numbers, the decimal numerical systems and the concept of zero. The Gupta Empire eventually collapsed in the sixth century largely due to invasions by the Huna people from central Asia.

THE QIN AND HAN DYNASTIES OF CHINA, AND CONFUCIUS

From around 485–221 BC, China was divided into several competing kingdoms and states (including that of Zhou – see page 23). Out of this rose the kingdom of Qin (from which the name China is derived), which in 221 BC formed China's first united empire.

The Qin emperor instituted a rigid form of government, and established a unified system of writing, weights and measures. Concerned about wandering tribes to the north, the Qin also created the Great Wall of China (linking earlier defensive walls) and ordered the construction of life-size statues of an entire army, known as the Terracotta army. The Qin dynasty lasted only to 207 BC, but during its brief rule it had established the approximate boundaries and basic administrative systems that are still a feature of modern-day China.

The much longer-reigning Han dynasty (206 BC–AD 220) firmly established Chinese culture (so much so that Han became the Chinese word for someone who was Chinese). The performing arts flourished, as did painting, sculpture and design, and huge advances were made in science and technology (innovations that were unknown to the western world for some time). Advances included the invention of paper, the sundial, the seismograph and compass. Han rulers extended the borders to take in Korea and parts of Vietnam, and further contact was made with the outside world, particularly along the 4,000-mile trade route known as the Silk Road along which, from around AD 100, Chinese merchants carried silks to the western world.

The Han continued the Qin's highly centralized form of government, although Han leaders were taught to respect the teachings of the great Chinese philosopher Confucius (*c.* 551–479 BC). Confucian ideology emphasized moderation and virtue over that of individual gain, and the possibility of shaping your own destiny, as embodied in a social code and philosophy that is still influential in China, Korea, Japan and Vietnam. From around AD 189, the Han Empire eventually fractured into regional regimes fought over by warlords.

EUROPE

THE ETRUSCANS AND THE FOUNDING OF ROME

The Etruscans were inhabitants of ancient Etruria (which roughly corresponds to modern-day Tuscany in Italy) who formed a loose alliance of Etruscan city-states. Etruscan culture developed in Italy from 800 BC onwards, and by the seventh and sixth centuries BC, the Etruscans dominated much of central Italy.

The origin of the Etruscan people remains a mystery, although one theory is that they came to Italy from Asia following the collapse of the Hittite Empire. The Etruscans used an alphabet derived from the Greek alphabet, although their language has not yet been translated. Rich archaeological remains, however, testify to a strong artistic tradition that included impressive bronze work, figurative sculptures, and art and architecture that greatly influenced Rome. The Etruscans were the first to lay out a city with a grid plan and allowed women to be freely involved in public life. They were also renowned as a strong maritime power.

By the end of the sixth century BC, however, the Etruscans were driven out of southern central Italy by the Greeks (who had established Magna Graecia in the south), as well as the ancient Indo-European tribes of the Latins and Samnites.

The city of Rome – which was founded, according to Roman tradition, in 753 BC – had been settled by several communities, including the Etruscans and Latins. Its first king and founding father Romulus was followed by another six kings who were of both Latin and Etruscan origin. Legend has it that in 509 BC, the tyrannical rule of Tarquinius Superbus led the people of Rome to expel him from the city, after which the Romans set up a republic.

In 474 BC Etruria's navy was defeated by a coalition of Magna Graecia cities at the Battle of Cumae. Thereafter, the Etruscan civilization suffered long decline until it was finally assimilated into the Roman Republic in the mid-third century BC.

ANCIENT GREECE AND THE BIRTH OF DEMOCRACY

The obscure years that followed the fall of the Mycenaean civilization eventually led to the emergence of powerful city-states in Greece. The cultural and scientific achievements of Ancient Greece would in turn spread across a vast empire and profoundly influence the Roman Empire, as well as Western civilization.

Beginning in around 730 BC, town life in Greece grew, as did overseas trade and agricultural production, all triggered in part by the rising power of the Assyrian Empire (see page 18) and its appetite for imported luxuries. These towns grew into powerful city-states, with Athens, Sparta, Corinth and Thebes emerging as the most dominant during Greece's Archaic period (650–480 BC). Often at war, these city-states met every four years at Greece's prestigious sporting event, the Olympic games. Increased trade led to a flexible writing system (by adapting and improving the Phoenician alphabet) and widespread literacy. The Archaic period of Greece also saw the creation of Homer's epic poems, the *Iliad* and the *Odyssey*, the development of Pythagoras's mathematical theory and the establishment of Greek colonies and trading centres as far away as Egypt, Byzantium and Syracuse in Sicily.

Classical Greece (*c.* 480–336 BC) is known as the greatest age of Greek history. Consisting of several hundred polis or city-states, it was ruled from the most powerful, Athens. During this period the Greeks repulsed Persian attempts to annex their land, most famously at the Battle of Marathon in 490 BC (see page 29), and the Parthenon was built in Athens in celebration. In the fifth century BC, Athens successfully repulsed a Spartan invasion; then in a bid to avoid tyrannical rule by local rich landowners, the people of Athens established the world's first democracy (from the Greek *demokratia*, 'rule of the people'), in which all citizens (bar women, slaves, children or foreigners) had equal rights – it should be remembered that this amounted to 85–90 per cent of the population.

In 431–404 BC, the Athens–Sparta Peloponnesian War

ended with Sparta the dominant force in the region, while Athens never regained its former prosperity. In 411 BC Athenian democracy was overthrown.

ALEXANDER THE GREAT AND THE HELLENISTIC PERIOD

The conquest of Greece in 339 BC by Philip II of Macedonia (a neighbouring kingdom ruled by a warrior aristocracy) marked the beginning of what was to become the Hellenistic Period in Greece (*c.* 323–30 BC).

An exceptional soldier, Philip II revolutionized warfare in Greece through the use of cavalry and siege warfare techniques (previously seen only in Assyria). Assassinated in 336 BC, Philip's dream for Macedonia to take over the Persian Empire was taken up by his twenty-year-old son Alexander III, student of the great Macedonian philosopher Aristotle, later to be known as Alexander the Great. Inheriting his father's fine army, Alexander embarked upon an eleven-year campaign that created the largest empire the world had yet seen (and firmly established himself as one of history's greatest military geniuses).

After his succession, Alexander invaded Persia and defeated King Darius at the Battle of Issus in 333 BC (thereby liberating the Greek cities in Anatolia). He then swept through Syria, destroyed Tyre and eventually conquered lands as far apart as Egypt and north-west India. The language and culture of Greece simultaneously spread throughout these vast territories and Alexandria (founded by Alexander in 332 BC) in Egypt and Antioch in Syria became the new centres of Hellenistic culture, while the Greek city-states declined in influence.

Following Alexander's death in 323 BC, much of the empire was carved up and ruled by Macedonian generals, to include Ptolemy (ruled 323– 285 BC) whose dynasty in Egypt lasted nearly 300 years until it was annexed by Rome (see page 14) in 30 BC, and Seleukos (ruled 312–281 BC), whose descendants ruled from Thrace in Europe to the border of India until the mid-second century BC when they were expelled by the Parthians (see page 29).

THE ROMAN REPUBLIC

By 509 BC, Rome had been established by its nobles as a republic (see page 42), ruled by two consuls elected by a Senate. The civilization that would emanate from this ancient city – its culture, language and technological achievements – would last for more than a thousand years and eventually spread across an empire that would encompass Europe, North Africa and the Middle East.

In the centuries after 509 BC, Rome grew in strength, defeating the Etruscans, Samnites and Greek settlers in Italy (and building the famous road, the Appian Way), eventually securing the Italian peninsula by 272 BC. Clashes with Carthage led to the Punic Wars (264–146 BC) and the emergence of the Carthaginian general Hannibal (see page 36). By 146 BC, however, the Romans had destroyed Carthage, and secured the overseas territories of Sicily, Spain and North Africa, and, through the four Macedonian Wars, extended its power into Macedonia, Greece and parts of Anatolia (although the mighty Parthians in Persia checked Rome's expansion in the east).

In 58–50 BC, the Roman general Julius Caesar conquered all of Gaul, his military successes resting not so much on his horsemanship and equipment as his tactics, discipline and military engineering. After a period of civil war in Rome, Caesar declared himself the republic's dictator for life. Senators responded by publicly stabbing him to death in 44 BC, which resulted in a further struggle for power, until Julius Caesar's adopted son Octavian defeated the general Mark Antony and Cleopatra at the Battle of Actium in 31 BC (annexing Egypt). In 27 BC, Octavian forced the Senate to award him a new name – Augustus, meaning 'augury', perhaps also linked to 'authority' – and, with the republic now defunct, he ruled (27 BC–AD 14) as Imperial Rome's first emperor.

THE ROMAN EMPIRE

The emergence of Imperial Rome bought with it peace and stability to the Roman Empire. Thousands of Roman troops guarded the empire's frontiers, whilst its emperors and administrators built a network of roads and constructed great towns and buildings, supported by elaborate water and plumbing systems. Legal administration and a common language (Latin in the west, and later Greek in the east) maintained unity in the empire, and Roman trade and influence spread beyond the empire's borders into India, Russia, Asia and along the Silk Road into China.

Roman emperors varied in capability, ranging from Claudius (AD 41–54), who conquered Britain in 43, and

Nero (AD 54–68), a cruel tyrant who ordered the burning of Christians, to Trajan (98–117), who expanded the empire to its greatest extent, and Hadrian (117–138), who limited further expansion by the construction of 'Hadrian's Wall' in the north of Britain. In AD 286, Emperor Diocletian split the empire into eastern and western halves for administrative purposes (they were still to be considered an undivided whole), and in 324 Emperor Constantine I retook control of the whole empire and established the Greek town of Byzantium as its capital (renaming it Constantinople and founding the Byzantine Empire – see page 59).

In the end, the empire's sheer size led to its downfall and from around AD 180 it entered a period of instability as its troops faced successive opposition from Europe and Asia (most notably in 260 when the Sāssānid Empire defeated and imprisoned Emperor Valerian at the Battle of Edessa). In 396 the empire was again divided into east and west, with the west increasingly weakened by battles with migrating settlers from central Europe. In the fifth century, Germanic tribes poured across the Rhine into the empire, sacking Rome three times. The Western Roman Empire finally collapsed in 476 following the abdication of the last Roman emperor, Romulus Augustulus.

THE CELTS

The Celts were a group of Indo-European tribes who by 500 BC lived in south-west Germany, north-east France (where they were known as the Gauls), and Bohemia. Skilled in horsemanship and metalwork, the Celts may have originally come from the Caspian Sea region, with the earliest known archaeological record – namely graves of Celtic chieftains in Hallstatt, Austria – dating to around 700 BC.

Excavations show that the Celts had one of the earliest Iron-Age cultures in Europe, and that they traded with Ancient Greece and Etruria. From around 400 BC, Celtic tribes advanced into Italy, settling in the Po valley and sacking Rome in around 390 BC. At the same time other Celtic tribes pushed south into France and Spain, east into Anatolia (where they founded Galatia) and west into the British Isles. Between the mid-fifth century BC and the first century BC, the Celts probably reached the height of their powers with the distinctive artistic style of La Tène culture (geometric patterns and stylized birds and animals) featuring in much of their jewellery and metalwork.

The Celts were largely a farming people (developing the ox-drawn plough in place of manual implements), who lived in well-defended villages and hilltop forts, and whose religious rites were conducted by a Druidic priesthood. They lacked, however, a writing system and political cohesion and the highly trained Roman legions, as well as the Germanic tribes, eventually overwhelmed them. Pockets of Celtic culture and language survived only on the fringes of Europe: in Brittany, Wales, Scotland, Ireland and the Isle of Man (Breton, Welsh, Scottish Gaelic and Irish are all Celtic languages in origin).

THE AMERICAS

PERUVIAN CULTURES

The Paracas culture, which was related to the Chavín civilization (see page 26) and located on a desert peninsula south of Lima, flourished from around 900 BC to AD 400. Much of what we know about the Paracas comes from excavations made in the 1920s at Cerro Colorado, where shaft tombs, each containing multiple bodies wrapped in intricately woven textiles, were unearthed. These revealed that the Paracas followed elaborate burial and mummification rituals, placing ceramics and other offerings alongside their dead and possibly drying or smoking the bodies to preserve them.

From around AD 100 to 800, another civilization, known as the Moche, emerged further north along the Peruvian coast at Sipan. They were particularly noted for their detailed painted ceramics (producing, for the first time, ceramic objects from moulds, enabling mass production of certain forms), gold metalworking, and monumental pyramid-like constructions known as huacas. The largest of these was the huacas del Sol, which at over 41 metres high, was the largest pre-Colombian structure in Peru. Moche culture was agriculturally based, and they developed sophisticated irrigation techniques and introduced the use of guano (sea bird excrement) as a soil fertilizer.

OTHER CULTURES IN THE AMERICAS

In North America, Stone Age nomadic life predominated, although in around 500 BC, new farming methods emerged, most notably in the region of the Ohio River valley. Here, the people of the Adena culture, who mainly subsisted on hunting and gathering, farmed a few local plants, including sunflowers, squash, and tobacco, for ceremonial purposes. They also constructed large earthen mounds, in which they buried their dead, as well as great animal-shaped earthworks, some of which, such as the Serpent mound in southern Ohio, still exist.

From around AD 200, Indians known as the Mogollon who lived in the mountains of south-eastern Arizona and south-western New Mexico began producing beautifully painted and well-crafted pottery. They lived in houses built half underground in small pueblo villages and obtained food principally by hunting and foraging. Their small communities lasted until around 1450.

Further south in Mexico, in around the eighth century BC, the hilltop city of Monte Alban in Oaxaca state began life as the centre of the ancient Zapotec culture. One of the earliest cities of Mesoamerica, it contains great plazas, underground passageways, courts for ball games and elaborate tombs. The city reached its peak in around AD 400–500 but was abandoned by 750.

CHAPTER THREE:
THE MIDDLE AGES
AD 450 to 1066

MIDDLE EAST AND AFRICA

AKSUM, THE GHANA EMPIRE AND THE MIGRATION OF THE BANTU

The African kingdom of Kush (see page 34) was overthrown in AD 300 by the great trading empire of Aksum, which was located in the north-east of the continent between the Red Sea and the Nile (Aksum is now a city of modern-day Ethiopia). Converting to Christianity in the fourth century AD, the Aksum Empire, which eventually encompassed several wealthy cities, remained an important commercial centre until the late 600s when it could no longer compete with the increasing influence of the Islamic Arabs in Mediterranean trade. Aksum is best known for its architecture, in particular its 126 huge obelisks, up to 34 metres high.

Another African nation (and the earliest recorded by the Arabs) was the Ghana Empire of western Africa, which arose in the eighth century. Unrelated to modern-day Ghana and situated in an area now occupied by part of Mali and south-eastern Mauritania, it developed into an important trading centre for gold, which was obtained in the south and exchanged with Arab traders for various commodities, including salt. Ghana declined in the 1000s with the rise of the Muslim Almoravids (see page 74).

The early history of African peoples further south is less well documented, although it's thought that the language and agriculture of Bantu-speaking people from eastern Nigeria had, by the beginning of the Christian era in Europe, spread southwards into southern Africa, displacing the hunting and foraging practices of its people. By the eighth century AD, towns on the east coast of Africa with links to kingdoms further inland had already been established by people who spoke what the Arabs later called Swahili (from the Arabic word meaning 'of the coast').

THE BIRTH OF ISLAM

In around AD 610, an Arab merchant living in Mecca, Muhammad, had a vision in which he was instructed to proclaim the greatness of One Almighty God, Allah. As he preached his message, he attracted supporters, although officials in Mecca viewed him as a dangerous enemy. Muhammad's escape from assassins to join his followers in Medina on 16 July 622, is known as the Migration – the 'Hegira' – and the Islamic calendar is dated from this year.

The teachings of Muhammad, known as Islam (meaning 'surrender' as believers surrender to the will of Allah) were later written down in the Qur'an. Muhammad returned to Mecca with a large army of followers, conquered the town, and later preached the message of Islam to a gathering of some 40,000 pilgrims (also urging them to pray five times a day, facing Mecca). His message spread rapidly, and by the time of his death in 632, most of the Arab peninsula was under Islamic rule.

Under the leadership of Muhammad's father-in-law Abū Bakr (known as the 'caliph', meaning successor or deputy) and the caliph Omar, the new faith of Islam was taken beyond the Arab peninsula into Palestine, Sāssānid Persia and Egypt. Thereafter Arab armies took control of the whole of North Africa, large parts of Asia (including western India) and from around 670 repeatedly attempted, without success, to conquer Constantinople. Cyprus and Sicily also fell to Islamic rule, as did Spain (previously under the Visigoths), although Arab armies were defeated by the Frankish ruler, Charles Martel, at Poitiers in 732.

By 751 the great Islamic Empire stretched from the borders of France to China, and the Holy cities of Mecca and Medina had become wealthy centres of sophisticated Arab culture, religion and Islamic law.

The Abbāsid Caliphate

During the Islamic conquests, new Islamic dynasties were set up, most notably the Omayyad dynasty, whose capital of Damascus in Syria became the centre of the Islamic Empire. In 750, descendants of the prophet Muhammad's uncle, the Abbāsids, overthrew the Omayyad dynasty, and in 762 moved the capital from Damascus to Baghdad, Iraq. (The Omayyad fled to Spain – Al-Andalus – where they established their dynasty in Córdoba in 756.) The Abbāsid caliphate focused more on the east – Iraq, Persia, India and central Asia – than North Africa and the Mediterranean, and Baghdad became a prosperous cultural, social and commercial centre of a huge trading empire.

Between 750 and 833, the Abbāsids raised the prestige and power of the empire, most famously under its fifth caliph Hārūn al-Rashīd, whose reign between 786 and 809 began what has been called 'the golden age of Islam'. His (some say overblown) reputation is largely the result of the literary masterpiece, *The Thousand and One Nights*, for which Hārūn al-Rashīd's lavish court provided the inspiration. His son, al-Ma'mun (reigned 813–33) was more successful in putting down rebellions in the empire and waging war against the Byzantines. He also built observatories for the study of astronomy and promoted the translation of Greek philosophical and scientific works (which greatly contributed to the revival of classic learning in Europe).

This revitalization in scholarly thought, which also absorbed the knowledge and skills of India, Greece, Persia and China, led to great advances in the realms of the arts, sciences, law, medicine, and agriculture. Arabic numerals, based on Indian numerals, are now commonly used around the world, as is the manufacture of paper, a Chinese invention improved by the Arabs. Other Islamic achievements include the development of trigonometry, as well as advances in optics, mathematics and astronomy.

THE FĀTIMID CALIPHATE

The Fātimid caliphate was founded in 909 in Tunisia by Abdullah al-Mahdī. As a Shi-ite Muslim, he claimed descent from Muhammad's daughter Fatima (descendants of whom, according to Shi-ites, are the only eligible successors to Muhammad, as opposed to Sunnis who believe any follower of Islam is entitled to succeed). A rival to the Sunnite caliphate of the Abbāsid dynasty, Fātimid influence soon extended over all of central Maghreb (an area encompassing modern-day Morocco, Tunisia, Algeria and Libya) from the newly built capital Mahdia in Tunisia.

In the late tenth century, the Fātimids, with the help of local mountain people, the Berbers, conquered Egypt, building the new capital of al-Qahirah (Cairo) in 969. There, the Fātimids commissioned the construction of the Al-Azhar Mosque, which developed into a university and, along with the library of Cairo, made the city a great centre of learning. The Fātimids were also known for their fine glassware, metalware and ceramics, and much of their architecture can be seen in Cairo today. At its peak (around 969), the Fātimid caliphate, with its centre in Egypt, ruled over an empire that encompassed North Africa, Sicily, Palestine, Jordan, Lebanon, Syria, parts of modern-day Saudi Arabia (including Mecca and Medina) and Yemen.

In 1057, a Fātimid caliphate was briefly proclaimed in Baghdad but thereafter the dynasty went into decline, as the Fātimids lost hold of much of their territory on the Levant and parts of Syria due to Turkish invasions and the Crusades. Dispute over succession led to their eventual collapse in 1171 when the caliphate was succeeded by the Sunnite Ayyubid caliphate, led by the legendary Kurdish Muslim, Saladin (see page 80).

FAR EAST

The Golden Age of China

The Tang dynasty in China (AD 618–907) and the short-lived Sui dynasty (589–618) followed nearly four centuries of civil war in China, during which time the Huns and Turks had invaded the north (between AD 317 and 589) and Buddhism had spread across its various kingdoms.

In contrast, the years of the Tang dynasty were relatively stable, with emperors ruling over a system of government that used loyal, trained officials rather than unruly nobles. Its capital Ch'ang-an (now X-ian) contained around 1 million inhabitants, an urban population that far exceeded any other in the world. Its large armies conscripted from China's vast population of around 50 million were able to dominate nomadic powers from central Asia and conquer or subdue several neighbouring regions, giving the Tang powerful cultural influence over Korea, Japan, south-east Asia and Tibet.

The Tang also reopened the lucrative trade route of the Silk Road, giving China direct access to Persia, the Middle East, India and central Asia. Its urban areas, in particular Ch'ang-an, absorbed much of this foreign influence and became cosmopolitan centres of commerce and craftsmanship. In turn, literature and the arts flourished, especially lyrical poetry, as well as ceramics (porcelain making its first appearance) and sculpture. Wood-block printing was also first introduced under the Tang, as was printing using moveable type, leading to the production of books centuries before anywhere else in the world.

From the eighth century, the dynasty began to weaken (beginning in 751 when Chinese forces were defeated by Arab armies and in 763 when Tibetan forces occupied Ch'ang-an). By the early tenth century, China was again divided into small states, until the Song dynasty succeeded in AD 960, which endured until the thirteenth century.

THE TAIKA REFORMS IN JAPAN

Emperors had ruled over Japan for many centuries, since, according to Japanese tradition, the fifth century BC, when the Yamato clan from south-central Honshu (around modern-day Kyōto) established power and loosely controlled much of the country.

From around the fifth century AD, China began to exert great influence, which affected Japan's system of government, religion, architecture and cultural practices. Buddhist teachings, brought to Japan by Chinese monks and adopted as the official religion in 538, marked a change in Japanese society. The ancient Japanese religion of Shintō – based on the worship of nature, spirits and ancestors, and through the supremacy of the Yamato clan, associated with the sun-goddess Amaterasu – was not destroyed, however, and co-existed alongside Buddhism in Japan.

In the seventh century, Prince Shōtoku Taishi (reigned 572–622) initiated a system of central government based on that of Sui China. In about 640 the Emperor Kotoku introduced further reforms (known as the 'Taika' reforms) specifically designed to organize the government along Chinese lines, by establishing a centralized civil service that would enhance the power of the imperial court. The new capital at Nara, built in the early eighth century, was also modelled closely on the Tang capital of Ch'ang-an. The cultural influence of China was felt at all levels: the Japanese adopted a modified form of Chinese as their official language and even the Japanese kimono is thought to resemble the clothing of China's Tang dynasty.

In 784 the Emperor Kammu moved the government to Heian (Kyōto), and thereon the Fujiwara clan ruled as civil regents (until about AD 1000) while the imperial family retreated into isolation.

THE GHAZNAVID EMPIRE

In 977 a former Turkish slave, Sebüktegin, became governor of Ghazna (modern-day Ghazni in Afghanistan), at that point under the control of the Samanid Empire in Persia. Sebüktegin later rejected Samanid control and with his son and successor he extended his rule over much of what is now Afghanistan.

In 998, the eldest son of Sebüktegin and the greatest of Ghaznavid rulers, Mahmud, made further conquests, capturing the Persian cities of Rayy and Hamadan, and expanding the empire so that it stretched from the Caspian Sea in the west to northern India in the east. Mahmud is reputed to have made many expeditions to India, where he ransacked and plundered temples and palaces and massacred huge numbers (50,000 Hindus on one raid). The city of Ghazna grew rich from these spoils and contemporaries marvelled at its ornate buildings, libraries and sumptuous court.

As this was an Islamic dynasty (the Ghaznavids having moved away from their pagan Turkish origins), Mahmud had also brought Islam to new frontiers, including India. After Mahmud's death in 1030, the empire began to fragment, largely as a result of the growing power of the Seljuk Turks (see page 78). As the empire contracted the Ghaznavids moved their capital to Lahore in the Punjab, and their power continued in north-western India until the Ghūrids (a Muslim dynasty from central Afghanistan) in 1186 seized Lahore and also burnt to the ground the city of Ghazna.

EUROPE

THE BYZANTINE EMPIRE

While Barbarian invaders ravaged the Western Roman Empire (see page 47), the Eastern Roman Empire and its capital of Constantinople (now Istanbul) thrived. Its first emperor Constantine (reigned AD 324–37) had promoted religious tolerance and made Christianity the Eastern Empire's official religion.

Straddled between Europe and Asia, Constantinople also became a hub of commercial activity between the two continents and beyond. This generated great wealth in the city and it became famed for its opulent art and architecture. Treasures from all over the world adorned its buildings, Greek and Roman culture – from literature to law – was preserved, while Christianity remained at the centre of Byzantine life.

Later emperors Theodosius II (408–50) and Anastasius (491–518) improved the finances and defences of the capital by building huge towers and fortified walls, and from 527 Justinian I rebuilt much of the capital. Intent on reuniting the east and west into a vast Christian domain, Justinian also expanded the empire by conquering North Africa and parts of Italy. He also collected and codified the laws of Rome, part of which still forms the basis of European law today. By Justinian's death in 565, the Byzantine Empire stretched from Spain to Persia.

In the seventh century, Muslim Arab forces swept through Persia, the Middle East, North Africa and into Spain, and between 674–78 they besieged Constantinople by land and sea but failed to take it. In the eighth and ninth centuries religious disunity, largely concerning the veneration of religious icons, weakened the empire. Thereon, theological differences between Constantinople and Rome led to the East-West Schism of 1054 (see page 68). The Byzantine Empire finally collapsed in 1453 when Constantinople was captured by the Ottoman Turks (see page 81).

BARBARIAN MIGRATIONS

From around AD 350, 'barbarian hordes' – which included the Indo-European tribes of the Goths and Vandals from the Lower Danube and Black Sea area – swept into Western Europe in search of new lands and wealth. Climatic change and an increase in population had driven them to migrate westward, as had the arrival of the Huns, a fearsome and nomadic race from central Asia who had conquered vast areas between the Rhine and Caspian Sea.

The onslaught of the barbarian people ultimately led to

the sack of Rome three times – firstly by the Gauls in 387, then by the Visigoths (Goths from Dacia, now in Romania) in 410 and finally by the Vandals in 455 – who stayed two weeks and took away artworks – leading to the collapse of the Roman Empire in Western Europe. Out of the turmoil emerged new kingdoms, including the Frankish kingdom in France (see page 64), and the settlement in England of the Angles, Saxons and Jutes from Germany and the Jutland peninsula. The Huns, however, having rampaged through Gaul and Italy, disappeared from view following the defeat and later death of their great leader Attila in 453.

In the following century, the Byzantines (see page 59) crushed both the Vandals in North Africa and the Ostrogoths (Goths from the Black Sea area) who had settled in Italy. The Visigoths who had occupied much of Spain were defeated first by the Franks in 507 and were then absorbed by Muslim invaders in the eighth century. The Germanic tribe of the Lombards, who had settled on the Hungarian Plains, invaded and occupied Italy in 568, and the Lombard kingdom remained independent until the Franks entered Italy in 773.

THE GROWTH OF CHRISTIANITY

The turbulent era of the barbarian migrations was accompanied in Western Europe by a gradual diffusion of Christianity. In around 500 the Italian St Benedict formed an early monastic community, in which monks devoted their lives to Christianity and lived by a strict set of rules (the Benedictine rule). By the early sixth century, Ireland was largely Christian thanks to the missionary zeal of St Patrick in the previous century, and by the late seventh century, Christianity had spread across Britain, instigated in part by the arrival of St Augustine of Canterbury (at the behest of Pope Gregory the Great) in England, St Colomba in Scotland and St David in Wales.

Monks then began to travel to Gaul and Germany, gradually converting their Germanic settlers who had originally worshipped their own pagan gods. Newly established monasteries also evolved into important centres of learning and craftsmanship, educating the young who lived nearby, copying down and preserving ancient Greek and Latin texts, creating beautiful illuminated manuscripts, producing fine objects in gold and silver whilst also cultivating the land around them and providing shelter for travellers and care for the sick. Monks also acted as advisers to the Christian leaders of the Frankish kingdom, who, as the empire extended across Western Europe and into central Europe (reaching its height under Charlemagne – see next page), consolidated the establishment of Christianity.

By AD 800 Western Europe was ruled entirely by Christian kings, and missionary activities (largely initiated by the Byzantine church) centred upon eastern and central Europe, to include the Christianization of the Slavic people in the ninth century, and the spread of Christianity into Russia in the late 980s (see page 67).

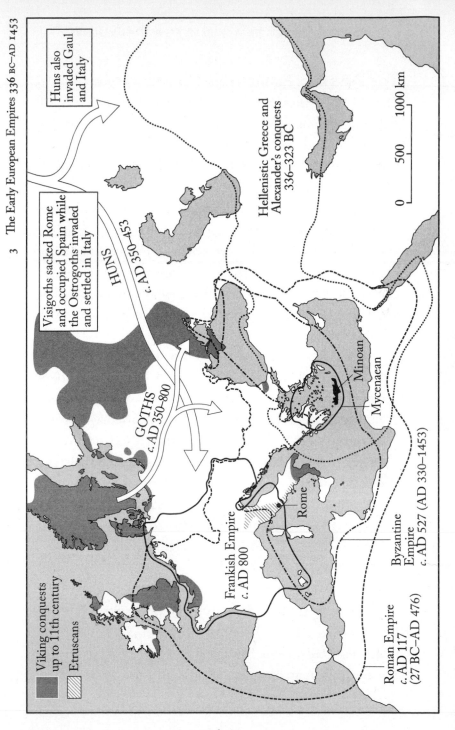

Huns also invaded Gaul and Italy

Visigoths sacked Rome and occupied Spain while the Ostrogoths invaded and settled in Italy

HUNS
c. AD 350–453

GOTHS
c. AD 350–800

Hellenistic Greece and Alexander's conquests 336–323 BC

Minoan

Mycenaean

Frankish Empire
c. AD 800

Rome

Byzantine Empire
c. AD 527 (AD 330–1453)

Roman Empire
c. AD 117
(27 BC–AD 476)

Viking conquests up to 11th century

Etruscans

0   500   1000 km

THE FRANKISH EMPIRE AND CHARLEMAGNE

The Franks were a warrior society based in modern-day Belgium, a group of whom moved to Gaul in France where they established the Merovingian dynasty. They were to have a greater influence on the shaping of Western Europe than any other barbarian people.

One of its more powerful leaders, Clovis, who had become ruler of the Western Franks in 481, converted to Christianity and brought most of what we now call France and half of Germany under his rule. The Merovingian dynasty gradually consolidated its hold over neighbouring kingdoms so that by the end of the eighth century, the Franks dominated much of Western Europe.

In 732, Arab armies entered France from Spain but were defeated by the Frankish leader, Charles Martel, at Poitiers, saving France and most of Western Europe from Arab dominance. In 768, Charles's grandson, Charlemagne, ruled over the Frankish Empire (also called the Carolingian Empire). In his zeal to Christianize Europe – and to defend and enrich his realm – he extended the empire to encompass part of Spain, Germany and much of Italy. In the east, Charlemagne also resoundingly defeated the Avars (Asiatic warriors similar to the Huns), subjugating some of the Slavs in the process.

Having helped to drive out the Lombards from Italy and restore its lands to the papacy, he was invited to Rome by Pope Leo III and crowned Holy Roman Emperor on Christmas Day, AD 800. This inaugurated what would become the Holy Roman Empire, which, as a union of central

European territories, formed a key driving force behind the Crusades (see pages 79–81).

A well-educated man, Charlemagne improved the legal system, encouraged education and promoted the arts and learning (leading to a revival of the arts in his court, known as the Carolingian Renaissance). After his death in 814, Charlemagne's empire fell apart after it was split between his three grandsons into the separate kingdoms of France, Italy and Germany.

THE VIKINGS

The Vikings were descendants of the barbarians who had settled in Scandinavia during the migratory period. From the eighth to the eleventh centuries, this formidable tribe of traders and pirates (the fiercest of them known as the 'beserkers') embarked upon an extraordinary period of expansion, attacking in their long ships the coast of Europe as far as Gibraltar and sailing vast distances across uncharted seas in their search for new land and trade.

In the ninth century, successive Viking raids on the British coast were fought off by the king of Dalriada, Kenneth MacAlpin, King Rhodri Mawr of Gwynedd and King Alfred of Wessex (rulers who then forged the kingdoms of Scotland, Wales and England respectively) so that Viking settlement in the British Isles was limited to northern England (the Danelaw) and the region around Dublin. But the Vikings continued to attack, and between 1016 and 1035 the Danish King Canute ruled England. It was only after his reign that Viking power was destroyed in England, and in Dublin the

threat did not end till the Battle of Clontarf in 1014.

Elsewhere in Europe the Vikings were able to strike far inland, sailing up main rivers (and dragging their ships short distances between rivers). They fought Europeans and Arabs in the Mediterranean and reached Constantinople by sailing down the rivers of western Russia, serving as mercenaries there. Sailing westward in their sturdy ships, they also made the first known voyages to Iceland, Greenland and North America (see page 106).

Where they settled, the Vikings generally lived as farmers and craftsmen, absorbing elements of the culture which they encountered whilst also bringing shipbuilding, navigation and trade knowledge, as well as fine decorative metalwork and the poetry of their epic sagas. In Normandy in northern France, Viking settlers merged with the Frankish population, and were later known as the Normans ('Northmen') who continued to have a powerful presence in Europe (see pages 93–4).

THE SLAVS AND MAGYARS

The Slavs were a broad group of peoples (whose history and origin are largely undocumented) who spoke a variety of Slavic languages of Indo-European descent.

Also known as the Antes or Venethi (among numerous other names), they migrated westward during the great migrations of the fifth and sixth centuries AD, settling in the regions of the Baltic, the Elbe, the Rhine (laying siege to Constantinople in AD 540), the Adriatic and the Black Sea. Thereafter, they established various Slavic states, to include the first Bulgarian Empire in AD 681 where the

Slavic language of Bulgarian was spoken. The missionary activities of Byzantium (namely by the brothers St Cyril and St Methodius, who are credited with having invented the earliest Slavic alphabet) led to the southern Slavs joining the Eastern Church in the ninth century.

The eastern Slavs occupied the river valleys of the Black Sea and the hills near Kiev, and their early settlements and towns formed the basis of future Russia. In the ninth century, the Vikings sailed up the long Russian rivers to conquer the eastern Slavs, selling some of them as slaves to the south (the name Slav eventually became synonymous with 'slave'). The Nordic and pagan influence of the Vikings continued for another century, although relations between Byzantium and Kiev strengthened steadily throughout the tenth century, culminating in AD 987 when the Russian prince Vladimir finally accepted Orthodox Christianity for himself and the Russian people (a turning point in Russian history and culture).

Another Eastern European people known as the Magyars who had in the ninth century settled in Hungary and Romania (from the area of the River Volga in Russia) advanced into central and Western Europe just as it was being plagued by Viking raids. In AD 955 they were finally defeated by the German king, Otto I, at the Battle of Lechfeld. Otto in turn conquered the lands from the Rhine to far beyond the Elbe (and overwhelming, also, the Slavs who lived there).

THE GREAT SCHISM

Increasing theological and political differences between the Byzantine Eastern Churches and the Western Roman Church led to a final and permanent separation between the two in 1054, a watershed in Church history known as the Great Schism (or East–West Schism).

The estrangement between Constantinople and Rome had been brewing ever since the division of the Roman Empire into east and west (see page 47) and the transfer of the capital from Rome to Constantinople in the fourth century. Constantinople's increasing power and its pre-eminence as the battleground between Islam and Christianity threatened the position of the Roman Church. And yet, unlike its Western counterpart, the Eastern Church was increasingly rocked by violent theological dispute amongst its patriarchates.

The cultural and linguistic differences of the east and west – Eastern theology had its roots in Greek philosophy, whereas Western theology was based on Roman law – increasingly led to a different understanding of Christian doctrine, most notably over papal primacy and the procession of the Holy Spirit from the Father and Son (the Roman Church incorporating the Son into their creed).

Matters came to a head in 1054 when Pope Leo IX and Patriarch of Constantinople Michael Cerularius suppressed Greek and Latin in their respective domains. This led to the two Churches, through their official representatives, excommunicating and denouncing each other. Constantinople later became known as the Eastern Orthodox Church; the

Western Church as the Roman Catholic Church, and the rift between the two has never been healed (although in recent years dialogue has been reopened, with the excommunications revoked by both Churches in 1965).

THE AMERICAS

THE MEXICAN CITY OF TEOTIHUACÁN AND THE EMPIRES OF HUARI AND TIAHUANACO

The first great city in the Americas, know as Teotihuacán (meaning 'City of the Gods') was built on the central plateau of Mexico 30 miles (48 km) north-east of where Mexico City stands today. At its peak, between AD 250 and 650, Teotihuacán housed over 150,000 inhabitants and covered an area of 8 square miles (21 square km). Built by the successors of the Olmecs (see pages 26–7), it was for two or three centuries a major religious and trading centre, trading, amongst other things, the green volcanic rock of obsidian to the Mayas (see pages 70–2).

Unlike other cities in the Americas, Teotihuacán was carefully planned around a grid pattern, containing multi-floor residential compounds, workshop areas, numerous squares, a ceremonial centre dominated by huge pyramids (the Pyramid of the Sun, at 210 metres across and 65 metres high, is the largest building of pre-Colombian Americas) and a central road lined with shrines and tombs, known as the Avenue of the Dead. Also notable in Teotihuacán are thousands of colourful murals, abstract depictions of mystical deities that adorn many of the city's shrines and houses. By AD 750 Teotihuacán had been destroyed, possibly by invaders travelling south into Mexico (later known as the Toltec – see page 72).

In the central Andean region, another ancient city in northern Peru, named Huari (or Wari), was discovered by archaeologists in 2008. With an estimated population of 100,000 people, Huari probably reached its greatest extent in the ninth century. It is closely linked in art style to the great monuments – in particular the solid stone arch, known as the Gateway of the Sun – found at Tiahuanaco, near Lake Titicaca, in north-western Bolivia. The two empires of Huari and Tiahuanaco probably controlled much of the central Andean region until they were both destroyed in the tenth century.

THE MAYA

The most advanced and long-lived civilization of pre-Colombian Americas was that of the Maya, based in southern Mexico and Guatemala.

Continuing some of the traditions of the neighbouring Olmec (such as temple building), the Maya reached its peak between the fourth and eighth centuries AD, although Mayan civilization, in the form of established towns and cities, dates back to around 600 BC.

During its peak, Mayan lands were divided between more than fifty city-states, each with populations ranging from 5,000 to 50,000. Whilst in frequent conflict, the cities were linked by good roads, shared a common cultural identity, and were ruled by a complex alliance of dynasties. The preeminent city was Tikal in the lowlands of Guatemala, except during a brief period from 378 when the Maya came under the influence of the Mexican city of Teotihuacán (see page 72).

Each city contained a king's palace as well as huge stone temples built on pyramids (possibly copied from temples in Teotihuacán), adorned with sculptures and colourful murals. Most of the Maya worked on the land, growing crops such as maize, in fields cleared from the rainforest (the Maya were unusual in that their civilization emerged out of rainforest rather than a floodplain).

From around AD 790, many of the Mayan lowland cities went into sudden decline, so that by 950 the population, which had numbered around 2 million, was reduced to a few tens of thousands. The reason for its sudden collapse is unexplained, although soil erosion may have been a factor. Mayan civilization survived in a diminished form in the Guatemalan highlands and the Yucatán peninsula of Mexico until the arrival of the conquistadores (see page 105) in the sixteenth century. Around 4 million descendants still speak a form of the Mayan language today.

MAYAN CULTURE

The ruins of the Maya reveal much about the extent and sophistication of their civilization, but it's only in the last thirty years, through the decoding of the Maya's complex writing system, that historians have gained a much greater insight into their achievements and belief systems.

Their language was written using hieroglyphs, either representing the abstract meaning of the object or concept, or the syllable of a word. As far as we know, the Mayan script was the only written language in pre-Colombian America that could represent all aspects of a spoken language. Thousands of books or codices made out of bound bark paper once existed but these were largely destroyed by the Spanish conquistadores (see page 105), so that now only four remain.

With expertise in mathematics and astronomy, the Maya also developed a sophisticated and complex calendar system. Like the people of Teotihuacán and many other pre-Colombian cultures, the Maya worshipped the jaguar, among dozens of other gods. Human sacrifice was also integral to their religious worship, and those who were sacrificed were assured an agreeable afterlife in the underworld. Ball games formed part of this sacrificial worship, and every Mayan city had a ball court, which represented the gateway to the underworld. Ball games often followed battles, after which the captives would be sacrificed to the gods.

The Toltec

The Toltec were a northern Mexican people who contributed to the downfall of Teotihuacán (see page 69) in the eigth century when they sacked and burnt the city under their leader, Mixcóatl ('Cloud Serpent').

Mixcóatl's son, Topiltzin, then founded the Toltec capital of Tollan ('Place of the Reeds') near modern-day Tula, approximately 50 miles (80 km) north of Mexico City. The city grew rapidly, with a palace complex at its centre, ball courts, and pyramid temples ornamented with huge stone figures, including one enormous temple dedicated to the chief god Quetzalcoatl. (Usually translated as 'Feathered Serpent', the image of Quetzalcoatl appears at Teotihuacán and throughout pre-Colombian Mexico.) Tollan eventually covered some 13 square miles (34 square km) and sustained a population of 30–60,000.

In the late tenth century, Topiltzin, along with fellow worshippers of the god Quetzalocatl, travelled east and settled in the former Mayan city of Chichen Itza, where they constructed buildings in the style of both the Maya and the Toltec. The Toltec were also noted for their fine metalwork and sculpture as well as the strange reclining stone figures, known as Chac Mool, found at Chichen Itza. These figures each had a dish resting on their stomachs, and it's thought they were used to hold the hearts of people sacrificed during religious ceremonies.

The Toltec were a warlike people, and after a series of military conquests in the eleventh and twelfth centuries, they held power throughout much of central Mexico. But in the mid-twelfth century they were eventually overrun by the nomadic Chichimec (Indian tribes from the north, who included the Aztecs – see page 102), who also ransacked and destroyed the city of Tollan.

CHAPTER FOUR:
WORLD ON THE MOVE
1050 to 1700

MIDDLE EAST AND AFRICA

THE ISLAMIC ALMORAVID AND ALMOHAD EMPIRES

The Almoravids were an Islamic Berber dynasty of Morocco who founded the city of Marrakech in 1062, and brought the regions of the western Sahara and part of western Algeria under their control. In 1075 they also conquered the Ghana Empire (see page 51) and then in 1086 defeated the Christian armies of Alfonso VI in Spain at the Battle of az-Zallaqah (Battle of Sagrajas).

By 1100 the Almoravids had control of all Muslim Spain (Al-Andalus) and their empire stretched some 3,000 miles (4,800 km) from Spain to Algeria in north-west Africa. Their supremacy, however, was short-lived after their king was murdered in 1147 by another Berber tribe from Morocco, the Almohads.

The Almohads seized control of Marrakesh, then the whole of Morocco, along with Algeria, Tunisia, Libya and Mauritania, and Muslim Spain. In 1172, in Spain, they transferred their capital to Seville and dominated Al-Andalus until 1212 when they were defeated by an alliance of Spanish and Portuguese princes at the Battle of Las Navas de Tolosa in the Sierra Morena. In 1236 and 1248 Córdoba and Seville fell to Christian power, and by 1248, the emirate of Granada was all that remained of Al-Andalus, ruled by the last Moorish dynasty of Spain, the Nasrid dynasty (the term Moor was principally used in reference to Berber people of African and Arab descent). In North Africa, the Almohads gradually lost their territories through local rebellion, enabling the Marīnid dynasty (a nomadic Moroccan tribe) to assume control of Morocco by 1269.

THE MALI AND SONGHAI EMPIRES OF WEST AFRICA

The decline of the Ghana Empire (see pages 51–2) led to the rise of the Madinka people of West Africa, who established in around 1230 one of the greatest trading empires in Africa, the Mali Empire.

The now Islamic state of Mali (following the nominal conversion of its founder and leader Sun Diata) soon controlled the lucrative caravan trade of the Sahara. With three huge gold mines to the south, it also became major suppliers of gold (providing half of the Old World's supply of gold), as well as salt. With efficient administration and a semi-professional army, the Mali Empire amassed great wealth and land, and at its peak in around 1350 the empire encompassed the whole of the Senegal Basin, running about 1,000 miles (1,600 km) inland, and ruling over 400 cities – at the time, only the Mongol Empire was larger. By around 1450, it had lost control of the trade routes and the Songhai (a former Muslim vassal state of the Mali Empire) had conquered its territories.

The Songhai's first emperor, Sonni 'Alī, who reigned from

1464 to 1492, soon took control of the remaining Mali Empire and its neighbouring kingdoms. In doing so, he secured several critical trade routes and cities, including Timbuktu in modern-day Mali, and continued to trade gold, which by the fifteenth century was in great demand in Europe. Under the Askia dynasty, ruled by Mohammed Turre, the Songhai Empire in the 1500s covered approximately 540,000 square miles (1.4 million square km), representing Africa's largest empire to date. Subsequent weak rulers, however, led to the empire foundering. By 1591 it was overrun by Moroccans, and in the seventeenth century the empire splintered into a number of smaller states.

West African Kingdoms, Great Zimbabwe and the Swahili Coast

The great empires of the Mali and Songhai were rivalled by other civilizations forming nearer the coast of West Africa. Two of these included the Yoruba city of Ife and the Edo city of Benin.

Ife, situated in south-western Nigeria, grew into a large settlement between the ninth and twelfth centuries. The city is known for its bronze, stone and terracotta sculptures, produced in great numbers between 1200 to 1400. Thereafter, political and economic power shifted to the nearby kingdom of Benin (in southern Nigeria), which by 1100 had grown into a major trading city, reaching its peak by around 1450. In the sixteenth and seventeenth centuries, Benin grew rich through the slave trade with the Portuguese and Dutch.

In southern Africa, the ancient palace city of Great

Zimbabwe had emerged from the eleventh century. Its position between gold and copper mines and the port was advantageous and its rulers had grown prosperous exporting as far away as India and China in return for Asian luxuries. This increasing wealth enabled the Shona people to create a rich and powerful empire, with the settlement of Great Zimbabwe as its capital. Reaching its greatest extent in 1450, Great Zimbabwe gradually declined due to the infertility of the surrounding lands, and after Portuguese incursions in the sixteenth century it was finally absorbed into the Zimbabwean Rozvi Empire in 1684.

On the East African coast, Arab settlements, which had first emerged from AD 700, still dominated trade, and between the eleventh and fifteenth centuries over thirty new Arab towns were built. The Swahili people (Bantu inhabitants living on the east coast) acted as intermediaries between the interior and ships arriving from India and China. With the money generated from this thriving trade, the Swahili established between the tenth and fifteenth centuries several city-states along the coast and on islands, all of which were Muslim and a combination of Arab and African styles.

PORTUGUESE EXPLORATION AND THE ADVENT OF THE ATLANTIC SLAVE TRADE

Throughout the fifteenth century, the Portuguese, in their search for sea routes to Asia, had explored the western coast of Africa. There, they established trading posts and initially exchanged goods with the kingdoms of West Africa on a relatively equal basis.

After Bartolomeu Dias rounded the southern tip of Africa in 1488, another Portuguese explorer, Vasco da Gama, opened up sea trade routes between Europe and the East. He made three voyages to India and became Governor of Portuguese India. Portugal had thus got to this lucrative market first.

During Europe's initial contact with Africa, few slaves were traded, certainly no more than had already been in existence elsewhere in the world (in the early Middle Ages, millions were enslaved by the Franks, Vikings, Arabs and Greeks). In the main, the Atlantic transportation of African slaves began in the late fourteenth and fifteenth centuries, as the Portuguese and Spanish, then Dutch, English and French established colonies in the New World. By the middle of the seventeenth century, more than forty slave fortresses were established on the west coast of Africa, where enslaved Africans brought in from the interior would be transported to colonies in the New World (a practice that would escalate markedly in the eighteenth century – see page 113). Between 1650 and 1850, 11.5 million Africans were transported.

THE SELJUK TURKS

In the mid-eleventh century a group of nomadic Muslim Turks, known as the Seljuks, moved down from central Asia (possibly as a result of the collapse of the Tang Empire in China) into Persia, evicting the Ghaznavids (see page 58) in the process. They then moved on to Baghdad where they were welcomed by the Abbāsid caliph, who made their leader Tughrïl Beg into his regent, naming him Sultan.

After occupying Syria and the Palestine, Tughrïl's nephew

Alp Arslan invaded Asia Minor and Armenia. In 1071 they resoundingly defeated the Byzantines at the Battle of Manzikert, during which the Byzantine emperor Romanos was captured, but later released. The Seljuks then began to settle in Asia Minor in large numbers, naming their settlement the Sultanate of Rûm (Arabic for 'Roman Empire', inferring they were the inheritors of the old Roman Empire). Large parts of Asia Minor were converted from Christianity to Islam, and Turkish gradually replaced the Greek language.

The Seljuks are also remembered as great patrons of literature and the arts, much of which combined central Asian, Islamic and Anatolian styles. The Persian mathematician and poet Omar Khayyám (1050–1123) – author of *The Rubáiyát* – lived under the Seljuks.

The threat to the Byzantine Empire and the capture of the holy land of Jerusalem (until 1098) led Pope Urban II to call for a holy war, or crusade, against the Seljuk Turks in 1095 (see below). During the first two crusades, the Seljuk Empire weakened (partly due to infighting amongst its principalities) and it eventually splintered into independent states during the Mongol invasions of the thirteenth century. In Asia Minor, one of these independent states – or 'emirates' – would later evolve into the great Ottoman Empire (see page 81).

THE CRUSADES

Pope Urban II's plea in 1095 to the nobility of Western Europe to recapture Palestine from the Muslim Turks led to almost two centuries of military campaigns in the Middle East, known as the Crusades.

Tales of Turkish atrocities – their desecration and plunder of the holy relics of Jerusalem – led thousands of Christians to take up the holy cause against the 'infidel'. Spiritual salvation was also promised, although commercial gain, in the form of land ownership, wealth and prestige, was increasingly a motivating factor among crusaders.

The first crusade was led by the Normans and included armies from France, Germany and southern Italy. After a two-year campaign, the city of Jerusalem was captured in 1099, after its Muslim inhabitants were massacred. The crusaders held Jerusalem for almost a century, until it was captured (along with most of the crusader holdings) in 1187 by Saladin, Sultan of Egypt, Syria, Yemen and Palestine. Shock in Europe over Saladin's victories prompted the third crusade, led by Philip II of France, Richard I (the Lionheart) of England and Frederick I Barbarossa. They succeeded in capturing Acre but failed to take Jerusalem, although merchants and unarmed pilgrims were allowed into Jerusalem whilst it remained under Muslim control.

During the fourth crusade, Venetian commercial interests led to crusaders sacking Constantinople; and in the sixth crusade, Jerusalem was recovered briefly, but lost again by 1244. In 1291, during the ninth crusade, the last remaining Christian fortress of Acre fell, marking the end of the crusaders' ambitions.

Despite 200 years of sporadic conflict most of Palestine remained in Muslim hands. Trade, however, flourished during the Crusades as exotic Middle Eastern goods as well as Arabic innovations and ideas, such as Arabic numerical figures and irrigation techniques, were brought to Europe. This stimulation of economic and cultural contact had huge benefits for European civilization, and contributed in part to the beginning of the Renaissance (see page 97).

The Rise of the Ottoman Empire

In an eastern emirate of Asia Minor, a prince (or 'beg') named Othman (whose descendants were called Othmanlis, or Ottomans, in the West) declared independence from the Seljuk Turks after 1293. With the aid of Islamic nomads fleeing the Mongol invasions, Othman gradually overpowered other Ghazi ('warrior') emirates in the region and introduced Islamic ideas of law and government. Thereon his successors took over most of Asia Minor and the Balkans.

The Ottoman conquest of Constantinople in 1453 marked a turning point in history, heralding the end of the Byzantine Empire and the beginning of a long period of Ottoman conquest, with Constantinople, now named Istanbul, as the Islamic capital. Selim the Grim (reigned 1512–20) added Egypt, Syria and part of Safavid Persia to the empire, and with Palestine and Greece, the Ottomans effectively ruled over what was the Roman Empire of the East.

Under Suleiman the Magnificent (1520–66), the empire reached its zenith. Suleiman pushed further into Europe and in 1526 he defeated Hungary and incorporated two-thirds of it into his empire (killing the king and almost every Hungarian nobleman in the process, and taking 100,000 prisoners). Known as the 'law-giver' in the East, Suleiman was also a noted administrator, reconstructing the legal system of the Ottomans and sponsoring the building of mosques, palaces, hospitals and schools. As a distinguished poet and goldsmith, he was also a great patron of the arts and culture within the empire.

With the help of the North African admiral, Khayr ad-Dīn (known as Barbarossa – 'red beard' – by Europeans), Suleiman dominated the eastern Mediterranean. By the mid-sixteenth century, the Ottoman Empire extended as far as Algeria in North Africa, and encompassed much of the Middle East and Eastern Europe (around 600,000 square miles or 1.6 million square km), representing the largest and most powerful empire in the world.

THE OTTOMAN EMPIRE: REVIVAL AND DECLINE

The first major defeat suffered by the Ottoman Empire occurred in 1571, off the coast of western Greece at the Battle of Lepanto. The fleet of the Holy League, made up of Venice, Spain, the papacy and Genoa, amongst others, inflicted serious damage on the Ottoman navy, destroying or capturing around 200 Turkish ships. While Christian powers believed this was a decisive blow for the Ottomans, the defeat had little long-term effect as the Ottomans simply rebuilt their navy and continued to control the eastern Mediterranean for another century.

Signs of fragmentation within the Ottoman Empire, however, were beginning to show when, under a series of weak sultans, the provinces began to assert themselves, although the Ottoman army was still sufficiently large enough to prevent rebels from assuming full control. Under Murad III

(1574–95) the empire even grew when Azerbaijan and the Caucasus were conquered, although early in the following century, these territories were lost, as was Iraq, and war with Venice between 1645–69 exposed Constantinople to an attack by the Venetian navy, though the Ottomans ultimately triumphed and retained Cyprus.

Next the Ottomans aspired to make strategic gains in the Austrian capital of Vienna, the centre of Europe. The turning point came in 1683, when an Ottoman army of 150,000 held the city under siege for three months, before they were forced to retreat by a combined European force, spearheaded by the Polish king Jan III. This marked the end of Ottoman advance into Europe.

Thereon, war with Europe led the Ottomans to lose many Eastern European territories. The Austrian Empire remained a serious threat, as did increasingly the Russian Empire, so that by the 1800s, the Ottoman Empire, once the mightiest power in the world, was jeeringly labelled by some as 'the sick man of Europe' (see pages 133, 147).

The Safavid Empire of Persia

The Safavid dynasty (1502–1736) was a relatively short-lived but hugely influential power in Persia. It brought Shia Islam to the region (where it still remains) and formed the foundation of the Iranian state with roughly the same boundaries as modern-day Iran.

The Safavids were from Ardabīl in present-day Iran, named after their founder Safī al-Dīn. In 1501, their leader Isma'il I made himself shah of Persia and over the next ten years subjugated the whole of Persia and the Iraqi provinces of Baghdad and Mosul. He also converted these largely Sunnite provinces to Shi-ism.

In 1514, Isma'il was defeated by the Ottoman Selim I (see page 81) and through continuing battle with the Sunnite Ottomans to the west and the Uzbeks to the east, the Safavids lost Baghdad and Kurdistan and their capital had to be moved to Esfahan in western Persia.

In 1588, one of the greatest shahs, Abbās I (reigned 1588–1629) took to the throne. He created a standing army, drove out the invading Uzbeks, regained the territory taken by the Ottomans and retook Baghdad. He also expelled Portuguese traders from the Persian Gulf and recaptured the island of Ormuz in 1622.

His military victories and effective administration enabled Abbās to unite the people of Persia. Trade with the West flourished, and through his encouragement of industry (to include the weaving of its famed carpets) and the arts, Persia acquired the status of a great power. Its capital Esfahān, with its great mosques, minarets and pavilions, grew into one of the most important architectural centres in the Islamic world. After Abbās's death, the Safavids went into slow decline, and were eventually conquered by Afghans in 1722, then Nadir Shah (see page 117) in 1736.

FAR EAST

A UNIFIED JAPAN

Since the twelfth century, Japan had been ruled by military leaders known as 'shōguns' (meaning 'great generals'), who in turn used warrior lords, samurai, to enforce law and order and govern large areas of land.

By the 1500s, the Ashikaga shōgunate had collapsed and Japan had descended into civil war as its great lords, the 'daimyō', fought for power. In 1543 Portuguese traders and Jesuit missionaries had arrived in the country, initiating for the first time commercial and cultural exchange between Japan and the West. Japanese rulers welcomed the arrival of the foreigners and were impressed by European technology and weaponry. A major daimyō named Oda Nobunaga used this new weaponry to overpower other daimyō, take the capital Kyōto in 1568 and in 1573 depose the last Ashikaga shōgun. Once in power, Nobunaga modernized his military forces, rebuilt roads and stimulated trade and business by prohibiting monopolies. Conversely, he is also remembered in Japan as a brutal figure who ordered the massacre of Buddhist warrior-monks who opposed him.

Nobunaga's forced suicide in 1582 (during an attack by a rebel lord) led to his general Toyotomi Hideyoshi taking power. By 1590 he had expanded his power and unified much of Japan. He invaded Korea twice but his armies were driven back by Korean and Chinese forces. Hideyoshi is also known for his cultural legacies, including the order that only the samurai could bear arms, and he even popularized the

Japanese tea ceremony as a way to talk business and politics.

After Hideyoshi's death in 1598, Tokugawa Ieyasu won the Battle of Sekigahara and established himself as shōgun in 1603, instituting the Tokugawa shōgunate at Edo (modern Tokyo), known as the Edo period, which lasted until the Meiji restoration in 1868 (see page 123). By 1639 all Europeans, bar a few Dutch, had been expelled and all Japanese were forbidden to leave the country, beginning two centuries of the 'Closed Country' period (*sakoku jidai*).

THE MONGOL EMPIRE

The Mongols were a nomadic tribe from central Asia who, with other Turkic groups, devastated much of Asia, Persia and southern Russia, to create one of the world's largest empires. The destruction bought about by the Mongols, and the millions who lost their lives, have been likened in scale to the Black Death and the world wars of the twentieth century.

The Mongols had threatened China for centuries but only under their leader Chengez Khan (in the West, Genghis Khan), meaning 'universal ruler', were they unified and powerful enough to capture Zhongdu (now Beijing) in 1215. Commanding a 130,000-strong army, Genghis Khan and his successors then turned west and conquered Persia, Armenia, northern India, European Russia and briefly Eastern Europe (including Poland and Hungary). They fought on horseback, and won battles through a combination of strategy, absolute ferocity and technology (they were the first people to use gunpowder in battle, as learnt from the Chinese, against European forces). Their savagery amounted to what many have described as genocide, particularly in the cities of Persia, Afghanistan and India where accounts speak of the annihilation of entire populations. In Mesopotamia, Mongol forces also destroyed the vital irrigation systems reducing their once fertile, flourishing provinces to desert (as it remains today).

After the death of Genghis Khan in 1227, the still expanding empire of the Mongols was divided between his sons and grandsons. One grandson, Kublai, defeated the Song dynasty to become China's first emperor of the Mongol dynasty in 1279. With the Silk Road trade route now within the sole rule of the Mongol Empire, trade between East and West flourished, and Kublai welcomed foreign merchants to China, including the Venetian Marco Polo who later astonished Europeans with his tales of a great civilization in the East.

The Mongol Empire, although devastating in terms of loss of life – some historians have estimated that around 30 million people died under the Mongols: China's population fell by half, and the Iranian plateau lost as much as three-quarters of its population – was thankfully short-lived, as quarrels over succession, incompetent administration and revolts led to its disintegration. By 1368 Ming forces (see page 91) had driven the Mongols out of China, and the vast domains of the Mongol Empire had largely broken apart.

THE TIMURID DYNASTY

Towards the end of the fourteenth century, a central Asian military leader who claimed descent from Genghis Khan, set out upon a series of bloody conquests in a bid to recreate the now-collapsed Mongol Empire. Named Timur-i-Lang (Timur 'the lame') or 'Tamerlane' in the West, his menacing force of skilled horsemen rampaged and slaughtered their way towards Asia Minor and back again, conquering Persia, Iraq, Syria, Afghanistan and part of Russia between 1364 and 1405.

Between 1386 and 1394 Tamerlane invaded Georgia and Armenia and enslaved around 60,000 people, and in 1398 he invaded India and massacred almost all of Delhi's inhabitants (where, it is said, the roads leading to Delhi were littered with corpses for months). In 1399, Tamerlane invaded Syria, killing the whole population of Damascus bar its artisans, whom he sent back to his capital of Samarkand (now in Uzbekistan). In 1401 he overran Baghdad where he massacred 20,000 Muslims. In 1402, Tamerlane invaded Asia Minor and defeated the Ottomans near Ankara.

His final goal was to conquer China and in 1404 he began preparations for a military campaign against the Ming dynasty, but died of fever and plague in 1405 on his way to the Chinese border. His brutal reign of terror had ended and his empire crumbled soon after his death. His most famed descendant was Bābur, who founded the Islamic Mughal Empire (see page 92).

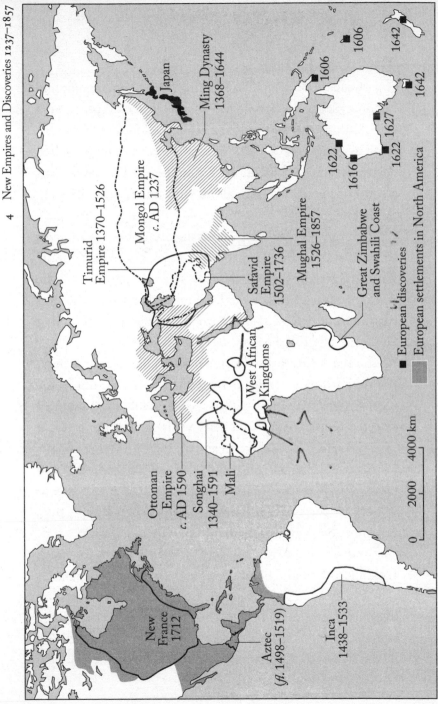

4　New Empires and Discoveries 1237–1857

Japan

Ming Dynasty
1368–1644

Mongol Empire
c. AD 1237

Timurid
Empire 1370–1526

Safavid
Empire
1502–1736

Mughal Empire
1526–1857

Great Zimbabwe
and Swahili Coast

1606

1606

1642

1642

1627

1622

1616

1622

■ European discoveries

　 European settlements in North America

Ottoman
Empire
c. AD 1590

Songhai
1340–1591

Mali

West African
Kingdoms

New France
1712

Aztec
(fl. 1498–1519)

Inca
1438–1533

0　　2000　　4000 km

THE BLACK DEATH

A particularly virulent and terrifying form of pneumonic and bubonic plague, known as the Black Death, swept through Asia, Europe and the Middle East in the fourteenth century. It led to a huge loss of life, with estimates of around 25 million deaths or more in Asia, another 25 million in Europe (at least a third of the population), along with unknown millions in the Middle East.

The origins of the plague are uncertain but it's thought to have started in the 1330s in the province of Yunnan, China. Spread by germ-bearing fleas living on rats, the disease rapidly spread through China and beyond its borders westward, carried by Mongol armies or merchants travelling along the Silk Road or on board sea vessels.

The Black Death first reached Europe in 1347 at around the time Mongol armies besieged the port of Caffa in the Crimea (where it's reported that Mongol soldiers catapulted infected corpses over Caffa's city walls). In the same year it spread to Italy (probably via ships), then to France, Spain, Portugal and England and on to Germany, Scandinavia and north-west Russia by 1351. In 1347, the plague also spread to various parts of the Middle East, first in Egypt, then Lebanon, Syria and Palestine, Iraq, Iran and Turkey.

The drastic population decline brought about by the Black Death also brought huge social and economic changes. A shortage of labour and more available land, particularly in Western Europe, increased the bargaining power of the peasant worker. Uprisings among the peasantry increased and by the sixteenth century, serfdom (a type of bonded labour) had largely disappeared in places like England, although it remained a feature of Eastern Europe and Russia, areas less affected by the Black Death.

THE MING DYNASTY IN CHINA

After the death of the emperor Kublai Khan in 1294, China was stricken by a number of natural calamities, including the Black Death (see previous page), which decimated its population and led to a series of peasant revolts.

One such revolt culminated in the establishment of the Ming dynasty ('Ming' means 'brightening') when Hungwu, a rebel military commander of humble origins, drove out the Mongols and set up a new dynasty at Nanking (now Nanjing) in 1368.

Hungwu set about establishing stable government and political unity. Farming improved, industry flourished, particularly in cloth-making and silk-weaving, and porcelain (known in Europe as 'china') began to be exported. In the first two centuries of Ming rule the economy boomed and the population doubled, and its leaders tried to improve the lot of the poor by abolishing slavery and increasing taxes raised from the rich.

Ming rule also saw the formation of a huge navy and standing army (of around a million troops) as well as large construction projects such as the imperial palace of the Forbidden City in the new capital of Peking (now Beijing). Trade with European powers was also encouraged, and between 1405–33 the Chinese admiral Zheng He led expeditions overseas, sailing vast fleets as far as the Swahili east coast of Africa and Jedda on the Red Sea. By the early fifteenth century, however, these maritime expeditions came to an end when an imperial decree forbade foreign voyage, and absolutism and isolationism became Ming hallmarks.

In the last century of the Ming dynasty, a succession of weak emperors, increasingly confined to their palaces, led to spreading corruption and infighting among court officials. In the 1590s treasury finances were depleted as China helped to drive back Japanese forces in Korea, while famine, drought, and a series of epidemics led to rebellion among the peasantry and in towns. In 1644, the Manchu, a warlike people from Manchuria, were asked to help restore order; instead they seized control of Peking and set up their own Qing dynasty (see page 118).

The Mughal Empire in India, and Sikhism

In 1526, Bābur, a Muslim Turkish descendant of Genghis Khan and Tamerlane (see pages 86, 88) marched into India, defeated the sultan of Delhi and conquered the central part of northern India. Bābur's territory – which also included the kingdom of Kabul in Afghanistan – came to be known as the Mughal Empire, a variation on the word 'Mongol', to reflect the emperor's ancestry.

Bābur was succeeded by a number of remarkable emperors, including: Akbar (reigned 1556–1605) who created a strong administration, allowed Hindus to worship freely and extended the Indian Empire so that it stretched from Gujarat in the west to Bengal in the east; and Shah Jahān (1628–58) whose court was the most magnificent of the Mughal Empire.

The introduction of Persian culture and language led to the emergence of a distinctive Indo-Muslim style in miniature painting and architecture, and to the adoption of the modern-day language of Urdu (which draws heavily from Persian and Arabic languages). Many of India's great palaces, tombs and forts are of Mughal origin, including the Taj Mahal in Agra and the Red Fort in Delhi, both built by the Emperor Shah Jahān.

In the early sixteenth century, a new monotheistic religion, Sikhism, grew in the Punjab area of India, founded by Guru Nanak. It combined elements of Hinduism and Islam, accepting the Hindu concept of karma and reincarnation but rejecting the caste system. The tenth and last guru, Gobind Rai (1666–1708), instructed that the surname Singh should be given to all baptized male Sikhs and prescribed the outward forms of Sikhism, such as long hair (to be covered by a turban) and an uncut beard. In response to Mughal hostility, he also militarized the Sikhs, who evolved into a potent political force in the Punjab.

EUROPE

FEUDALISM AND THE NORMAN CONQUESTS
In Europe, the political and economic system of feudalism – which was based around the holding of land in return for loyalty or military service – formed the building blocks of government and everyday life. Between the fifth and twelfth centuries it had spread from the Frankish kingdoms of France to much of Western Europe.

Here, kings leased land known as 'fiefs' to powerful lords or vassals in return for their allegiance. The lords, or religious institutions, then divided their lands into manors or estates for which lesser nobles or tenants were obliged to pay homage. At the bottom of the heap was a class of bonded peasants (serfs or villeins) who lived entirely under the jurisdiction of their master. Out of this system grew fortified castles (as it was necessary for lords to defend their domains), knights and a code of behaviour known as chivalry.

In 1066, the Normans, who had settled in northern France, defeated the English King Harold II at the Battle of Hastings and replaced the Anglo-Saxons as the ruling class in England. Their leader William ('the Conqueror') set up a particularly efficient feudal system, drawing up a list of every property and village in the land (as written in the *Domesday Book*), which he then bestowed to his nobility as 'fiefs'. The Normans also went on to conquer Wales, parts of Ireland and Scotland, and under their great leader, Robert Guiscard, they fought the Arabs and Byzantines and conquered Sicily and southern Italy.

From around the 1400s onwards, the feudal system in Western Europe began to fragment, partly in response to population decline brought about by the Black Death as well as the growth of commerce (see pages 95–6). In central and Eastern Europe, however, the institution of serfdom – bonded labour that underpinned feudalism – persisted well into the mid-nineteenth century.

THE GROWTH OF COMMERCE

From around the eleventh and twelfth centuries, trade increased in Europe, stimulated in part by the Crusades, improvements in roads and shipping, and the establishment of the Mongol Empire, which had opened up trade routes between East and West.

Towns and cities began to grow around areas of production and commerce: the ports of Venice (probably the richest city in Europe in the medieval period), Pisa and Genoa in Italy and Lübeck and Danzig in Germany became major centres of imports, and Bruges, Ghent and Ypres in Flanders and the Tuscan city of Florence dominated the cloth industry (Europe's most important export). The need for towns to control and regulate their own economic affairs led to the establishment of craft guilds and many towns and cities gained independence from their local lords (in Italy and Germany large towns were often ruled by rich merchants, rather than local nobility).

In northern Germany, the towns of Hamburg and Lübeck formed a trading alliance in 1241. At its height in the fourteenth century about 100 towns – from Bruges in Flanders to Kiev in Russia – had joined the commercial and defensive alliance known as the Hanseatic League. Formed chiefly to protect trading interests, the league would later evolve into an independent political power and retain its own army and navy.

The development of banking, notably in fourteenth century Florence (and later in Germany, Poland, Holland and England), also facilitated the growth of trade in Europe as merchants could buy and sell on credit. The wider circulation of money, the growth in commerce and the emergence of self-governing towns and cities all led to an erosion of the feudal system in Western Europe.

THE HUNDRED YEARS WAR

Fought between France and England, the Hundred Years War (1337–1453) lasted with some interruptions for 116 years, through the reigns of five English kings (Edward III to Henry V) and five French kings (Philip VI to Charles VI). The trigger for war was largely feudal: Edward III, as the Duke of Aquitaine, resented paying homage to the French king, and also claimed the throne of France. Rivalry over the lucrative Flanders wool trade also led to hostilities. At the outset of war, the English gained the upper hand and in 1346 Edward defeated Philip VI at Crécy, aided by his son, the Black Prince (named after the colour of armour), and the new English weapon, the longbow. The outbreak of the Black Death in 1347 resulted in a decade-long break in fighting.

In 1360, after several defeats, Edward III gave up his claim to the French throne in return for Aquitaine, although by the time of Edward's death in 1377, more territory had been lost to the new French king Charles V. After Charles V's death in 1380, the war then languished until Henry V ascended the English throne in 1413. He renewed his claim to the French throne and famously defeated the French at the Battle of Agincourt in 1415 (as immortalized in Shakespeare's *Henry V*).

After Henry V's death in 1422, the English under the Duke of Bedford secured several successes until the turning point

came in 1429, when Joan of Arc, the 'maid of Orléans', helped the French forces break the English siege at Orléans. Joan of Arc was burnt at the stake by English and Burgundian forces, but the French, with renewed nationalistic fervour, gradually won back their territory so that by 1453 only Calais and the Channel Islands remained under English rule. The French monarchy, with much of its nobility wiped out by the wars, went on to establish centralized power throughout the nation. However England's monarchs continued to claim the title 'King of France' until 1801.

THE RENAISSANCE

In Europe, increased contact with the Far East and the Muslim worlds stimulated new learning and thought, and an interest in the culture and values of ancient Greece and Rome. This artistic and intellectual awakening – known as the Renaissance, meaning 'rebirth' – emerged in Italy in the fourteenth century. During this time, Renaissance scholars recovered and studied classical texts (many of which came from the Arabic world via Muslim Spain and Byzantium).

The Renaissance also enriched the school of thought known as humanism, which placed greater importance on the abilities of the individual rather than on the divine or supernatural. Artists like Botticelli and Michelangelo began to represent the human form with greater realism, whilst Italian poets such as Dante and Petrarch explored human nature. Architects like Brunelleschi and Palladio created buildings that could be compared with the finest examples of the ancient world, and the artist, sculptor, engineer and

master of numerous other disciplines, Leonardo da Vinci, provided the archetype of the Renaissance Man. Rich and powerful families, such as the Medici in Florence, provided the financial backing for many of the Renaissance's artistic and technical achievements.

From around 1500, the Renaissance spread to northern Europe, where it took on a more religious character. The Dutch scholar Erasmus formed a new Christian humanism through his study of the original Greek New Testament, and his criticisms of the Church helped to foster the Protestant Reformation (see below). Crucial to the free circulation of ideas in Europe was the invention of the mechanical printing press by Gutenberg in 1450, although the Chinese and Arabs had made advances in printing and paper production many centuries earlier.

THE PROTESTANT REFORMATION AND COUNTER-REFORMATION

Widespread discontent with the power and corruption of the Roman Catholic Church, fuelled by debate among Renaissance scholars over its doctrine, led to much of northern Europe breaking away from the established Church in favour of something more evangelical.

This movement, known as the Protestant Reformation, is said to have begun in 1517 when the German friar and scholar Martin Luther launched a protest against the corruptions of the Roman Catholic Church. He later went on to translate the Bible into German and attack the Catholic doctrines of transubstantiation, clerical celibacy and papal supremacy.

Aided by Gutenberg's printing presses, Luther's ideas swept through Europe so that by 1530 Sweden, Denmark and parts of Germany had broken with the Catholic Church. England under Henry VIII followed suit in 1534. In Switzerland, a form of Protestantism became the dominant religion under the leadership of John Calvin, whose doctrinal revolution – later known as Calvinism – spread to western Germany, France, the Netherlands and Scotland.

The Catholic Church responded with its own reforms (known as Counter-Reformation), much of it spearheaded by the new religious order, the Society of Jesus (Jesuits). A great gathering of the Catholic Church, the Council of Trent (1545–63), clarified the doctrines of the Church, instituted important moral and disciplinary reforms and rejected all compromise with the Protestant faith.

The ensuing division between Catholics (still the predominant Church in southern Europe) and Protestants led to a series of European wars. In France, a bloody civil war between Protestants (known as Huguenots) and Catholics eventually led to religious toleration via the Edict of Nantes of 1598. However, Europe's most powerful ruler, Philip II of Spain, sought to restore Catholicism in Europe by force and a bitter struggle erupted in the Netherlands between Protestant rebels and Spanish forces, culminating in 1609 with the Dutch freeing themselves from Spanish Catholic rule. The ensuing Thirty Years War (1618–48), which began as a war between Protestant German princes and the Catholic Holy Roman Emperor, effectively ended in stalemate (Catholic states remained Catholic and Protestant *really ?*

states retained independence) and brought an end to the Counter-Reformation period. Meanwhile the ongoing Christian–Muslim conflict continued, with Philip II in a holy alliance with the Venetians destroying the Ottoman fleet at the Battle of Lepanto in 1571.

EUROPEAN EXPLORATION AND TRADING EMPIRES

The sixteenth century saw the beginning of the great age of European exploration, sparked in part by better shipbuilding and navigation techniques, and the need to find new trade routes that circumvented the expanding Ottoman Empire (see pages 81–2).

The seafaring nation of Portugal led the way, pioneering the sea route to the East Indies in 1498, sailing to the Americas, and establishing a string of trading posts off the coast of Africa, as well as in Macao, China and Goa in India. Spain also explored the seas, notably with the Genoese Christopher Columbus (see page 105) and then in 1520 when the Portuguese explorer Ferdinand Magellan (sailing under a Spanish flag) discovered a route to circumnavigate the globe. Spain's subsequent conquests in the West Indies and central and southern America (see pages 105–6) made her by the end of the sixteenth century the richest nation in Europe.

By the seventeenth century, the English and the Dutch were ready to rival the trading monopolies of the Spanish and Portuguese. English fleets sailed to North America and throughout the 1600s set up settlements in New England and Virginia (see pages 107–8), as well as in the West Indies. In 1600 London merchants set up the East India Company, initially formed to trade with the East Indies. In 1670 the Hudson's Bay Company in Canada was incorporated by royal charter, and controlled the fur trade throughout much of British-controlled North America for several centuries.

In 1602, the Dutch founded the Dutch East India Company and thereon built up a large and hugely profitable trading empire. They gradually overtook Portugal in the silk and spice trade, seizing various trading posts from the Portuguese in the East Indies and Asia. (In 1652 the Dutch Empire had also established a settlement at Cape Town in South Africa, as well as colonies in the West Indies and briefly in Brazil.) During the 1600s, France also acquired substantial territories in North America and Canada, the Caribbean and India.

Absolute Monarchy: Charles I and Louis XIV

The British monarch, Charles I (reigned 1625–49) believed, like his father, James I, before him that he had a God-given right to rule, that a king was, in essence, God's representative on earth. This, combined with Charles's apparent support for Catholicism, brought him into conflict with his Parliament and Puritan ministers.

Civil war erupted in 1642, with the armies of the Parliament (known as Roundheads) defeating the armies of the king (known as the Cavaliers). Charles's execution in 1649 led to the establishment of a republic under the leadership of Parliament's leading general, Oliver Cromwell. After Cromwell's death, Charles's son returned to the throne in 1660, to be crowned Charles II. Trouble again blew up under the Catholic monarchy of James II (reigned 1685–8) who, during the 'Glorious Revolution' of 1688, was deposed by Parliamentarians in favour of the Protestant rulers William III and Mary II. In 1689, Parliament drew up the Bill of Rights, a document that established the rights of Parliament and the limits of sovereign power, and which later influenced constitutional law around the world (including the United States Bill of Rights).

In contrast to Charles I, the French monarch Louis XIV (reigned 1643–1715) faced little opposition to absolute rule. On his accession, France was the most powerful country in Europe (thanks largely to the minister Cardinal Richelieu and his successor Mazarin, as well as the Thirty Years War which had reduced the once-mighty Spain to poverty). Known as the Sun King (as if he was the God-given sun itself), Louis largely ignored all representative institutions and excluded most of his great nobles from political office. From his lavish palace at Versailles, however, he succeeded in pacifying the aristocracy, eliminating any remnants of feudalism that remained in France, and consolidating a system of absolute rule that would endure until the French Revolution (see page 128).

THE AMERICAS

AZTECS

In the fifteenth and early sixteenth centuries, the Aztec people controlled a vast empire in what is now central and southern Mexico. Originally a nomadic people from the north, it's thought they arrived in the Valley of Mexico in the thirteenth century. There they settled on islands in the Valley's shallow lakes and began to build a city, Tenochtitlán (on a site that is now Mexico City).

Under the Aztec ruler Itzcoatl (who ruled 1428–40), Tenochtitlán formed an alliance with two neighbouring states to become the predominant power in central Mexico. Further conquests and commerce led to Tenochtitlán ruling an empire that encompassed 400–500 small states, with around 5–6 million citizens.

The Aztec economy was based on agriculture although they were also craftspeople and traders, operating a network of trade caravans across the empire. They were skilled sculptors, carving huge human-like figures out of stone, and also built splendid palaces, temples and pyramids, including the grand palace of Montezuma II (ruled 1502–1520) in Tenochtitlán. The Aztecs had no alphabet but used picture writing and hieroglyphics to record their history. Their language was related to the Native American languages of North America, and many Aztec words have been incorporated into Spanish, and even English (such as tomato, chocolate and avocado).

Religion was a great controlling force for the Aztecs and their priests kept an exact solar calendar (as learned from the Maya). The Aztecs believed the world would one day be destroyed, and to postpone this event and appease their various gods, they performed elaborate rituals, including human sacrifice, regularly sacrificing thousands of prisoners captured in war. (In 1487, an estimated 80,000 people were sacrificed to consecrate one temple.) The Spanish, when they arrived in Tenochtitlán in 1519 (see page 105), were horrified by these bloody rituals and destroyed many of the Aztec temples. Tenochtitlán was also destroyed, many Aztecs were tortured, killed or enslaved by their Spanish rulers, and the Aztec Empire collapsed.

THE INCA

The last and greatest civilization of pre-Colombian South America was the empire of the Incas. Its well-run central administration ruled over 5–10 million people and reached across almost all of the Andean region.

The Inca first formed a state around their capital Cuzco, eventually conquering the rival Peruvian state of Chimu. Its ruling dynasty was established in around 1200, and under Pachacuti Inca Yupanqui (ruled 1438–71) a series of conquests led to an expansion of the Inca Empire into northern Ecuador, across Peru to Bolivia and including, from around 1529, parts of northern Argentina and Chile.

Pachacuti and his successors also developed a highly efficient form of centralized government, underpinned by a rigid social hierarchy. This central administration controlled the building of new towns and even the production of art and pottery. Without any writing system, however, the Inca developed a string and knot device called a quipu, which stored information and lists.

Inca technology was of a high standard with workshops and factories producing metal artefacts, textiles and ceramics. The Inca also built a vast network of roads (at around 15,500 miles or 25,000 km, it was second only in size among ancient civilizations to the Roman Empire). As the wheel had not been invented, the Inca employed a system of couriers and runners to relay messages. Agriculture was based on hillside terracing and Inca religion centred on the official state cult of the sun-god Init. Many temples and shrines were built although these were not places of public worship as the Incas performed most religious ceremonies outside. In contrast to the Aztecs, they only performed human sacrifice on the accession of rulers.

From around 1525 civil war broke out in the Inca Empire, just before Spanish troops arrived on the coast led by Francisco Pizarro. The Inca ruler Atahualpa was executed in 1533 after being duped into supplying the Spanish with a huge ransom of gold and silver, Cuzco was captured, and by 1537 the Inca Empire had disintegrated.

THE CONQUISTADORES

In November 1519, a Spanish official named Hernán Cortés (1485–1547) arrived in Mexico with an expeditionary force of around 400 men. He had sailed from Cuba, where, some twenty-five years earlier in 1492, the Genoese sailor Christopher Columbus (under the support of the Spanish crown) had first landed before sailing in later voyages to central and southern America.

As Cortés' army moved toward the city of Tenochtitlán, local people, already resentful of Aztec rule, rallied to the Spanish army. After the Aztec ruler Montezuma was taken captive, full-scale war ensued during which the Spanish slaughtered hundreds of the Aztec nobility. Montezuma was also killed, and Cortés became governor of the renamed 'New Spain'.

Lured by the promise of great wealth, the Spanish explored 'New Spain' in search of a legendary 'city of gold', 'El Dorado'. They never found it but they did find silver in Peru and Mexico, which they shipped back to Spain (making Spain the wealthiest and most powerful country in Europe).

The Spanish settlers brought with them a host of European diseases, such as smallpox and influenza, which decimated the population of the Americas, and millions were also worked to death in the silver mines and agricultural plantations. The ensuing loss of life exceeded levels even of the Black Death: between 1492 and 1650, it has been estimated that the indigenous population of the Americas declined by 80–90 per cent. And as labourers died, African slaves were brought in to replace them, supplied largely by the Portuguese who had themselves conquered Brazil in 1500.

New France

The North American country of Canada was originally inhabited by Native Americans and Inuit in the far north. The first known Europeans to reach the continent were the Vikings who settled briefly on the northern tip of Newfoundland in AD 1000. Some five centuries later, in 1497, the island was next reached by the Italian navigator John Cabot (sailing under an English flag).

In 1534, it was the turn of the French explorer, Jacques Cartier, who tried unsuccessfully to set up a French colony in the area of the St Lawrence River. In 1583 the English adventurer Sir Humphrey Gilbert set up England's first

North American colony in St John's, Newfoundland. French fur traders eventually settled in Acadia in 1604 and in 1608 the French explorer Samuel de Champlain set up a trading station on the St Lawrence River, which grew into the city of Quebec. Fur traders and Catholic missionaries explored the Great Lakes and Hudson Bay and in 1682, the French explorer de La Salle followed the Mississippi River to its mouth, taking possession of its whole valley and naming it Louisiana in honour of the French king, Louis XIV.

The name Canada came to be used interchangeably with 'New France'. In the mid-seventeenth century, a brutal series of conflicts, known as the Beaver Wars (or Iroquois wars), broke out between the native Iroquois who sought to monopolise the fur trade and the French-backed Algonquian-speaking tribes. Later in the century, Anglo–French conflict in Europe led to four intercolonial wars (1688–1763), during which New France and New England fought each other with their respective Indian allies. By 1713, France was forced to give up to the British most of Acadia, Newfoundland and Hudson Bay and the remainder of New France was ceded to Britain and Spain after the Seven Years War in 1763.

EUROPEAN SETTLEMENTS IN NORTH AMERICA

The first English colony in North America was founded in 1607 in Jamestown, Virginia ('Jamestown' after the English monarch James I, and 'Virginia' in honour of Queen Elizabeth I, as named by Walter Raleigh, who had attempted and failed to establish a colony there in 1584).

Life for the colonists was perilous: more than 80 per cent

of them died during the winter of 1609–10. Native Americans – the Powhatan – initially shared food with the new settlers, but relations eventually deteriorated into mutual distrust and conflict. The settlement at Virginia increasingly relied on the cultivation of tobacco, first by indentured servants and then by African slaves first brought into the region in 1619.

In 1620, Plymouth, in what is now Massachusetts, was settled by Protestant separatists who had sailed on the *Mayflower*. Conditions were similarly hard but roughly half the settlers survived the first winter, largely through the support of Native Americans. In 1629 more English Puritans arrived and the colony prospered.

Between 1623 and 1732 a string of English colonies were established on the eastern seaboard of North America, from New Hampshire to South Carolina. Settlers from other European nations also arrived in the seventeenth century, including the Dutch who established a colony in 1624, naming it New Amsterdam (today, New York), capital of New Netherland, as well as the Swedes who settled in Delaware in 1638, both of which fell to the English in the 1660s. Germans also settled in Pennsylvania and Georgia, and a host of other nations, including Scandinavians, Swedes, Poles, Irish, Italians and French added to the cultural diversity of the settlers, while ships continued to bring slaves from the west coast of Africa (see pages 78, 113).

OCEANIA

European Discoveries of the Pacific Lands

The islands of the central and southern Pacific Ocean had been settled by the Polynesians (who may have originally come from Indonesia) between 2,500 and 1,500 BC. The Polynesians were skilled navigators, and by AD 400–500 they had reached the majority of Polynesia's islands, many of which – including Tonga, Samoa, Tahiti and the Hawaiian islands – developed into advanced societies, despite being cut off from much of the world.

Europeans first made contact with the Pacific lands in the sixteenth century. In 1511 the Portuguese reached Malacca in Malaysia, and in the following year, they arrived on the famous 'Spice Islands' in the Moluccas and also took Makassar in Indonesia and Timor in 1514. Later Portuguese ships reached New Guinea in 1527. In 1521, the Portuguese navigator Ferdinand Magellan, sailing with a fleet of three Spanish ships, reached Guam and the Philippines, and on their return to Spain (without Magellan, who had been killed in the Philippines) the fleet completed the first maritime voyage around the world.

The remote island of New Zealand was first settled by the Maori in the early thirteenth century. Originally sailing from Polynesia in large canoes, over the subsequent centuries a distinctive Maori culture was established. The first European to reach New Zealand was the Dutch explorer Abel Tasman in 1642 (also reaching Tasmania, which was named after him).

The first recorded European sightings of Australia, which had been inhabited by the Aborigines for some 50,000 years, occurred in the seventeenth century. The Dutch navigator Willem Janszoon reached the Cape York Peninsula in 1606, and throughout the century, the Dutch charted the western and northern coastline (of a land they called 'New Holland') but made no attempts at settlement. An English explorer and privateer, William Dampier, landed on the north-west coast in 1688 and again in 1699, but it wasn't until the eighteenth century that more permanent settlement would be attempted (see page 142).

CHAPTER FIVE:
REVOLUTION AND EUROPEAN IMPERIALISM

1700 to 1900

MIDDLE EAST AND AFRICA

THE OYO AND ASHANTI EMPIRES

The slave trade in Africa continued to expand throughout the eighteenth century (see page 113). Small African states that lay near to the western coast served as suppliers to the Europeans and grew into sizeable empires.

The Yoruba kingdom of Oyo, situated in present-day south-western Nigeria and southern Benin, had by the eighteenth century expanded to the south-west, thereby securing a trade route to the coast and the Atlantic slave trade. Conquered people from newly acquired territories, including the Kingdom of Dahomey, were traded with the Europeans or used as slave labour on royal farms. To govern its territorial domains, the Oyo also developed a highly sophisticated political structure. The empire fell in the early nineteenth century as a result of local revolts, foreign incursions and a decline in the demand for slaves.

The Ashanti Empire controlled what is now southern Ghana, Togo and Côte d'Ivoire in the eighteenth and nineteenth centuries. Its wealth was based on trade in gold and slaves, which it exchanged with British and Dutch traders for firearms. Its territory, which included states formerly subject to the Denkyira kingdom, had a population of 3–5 million, governed by a strong central administration at Kumasi. Kumasi also became an artistic centre for the production of ornate gold and silver ornaments.

In the nineteenth century, the Ashanti fought a series of military campaigns against the colonial power of Great Britain, which sought to strengthen its position in West Africa. Early successes against the British army were followed by a reversal of fortune in 1826 and further territorial losses to the British. By 1902, the Ashanti Empire had become subsumed in the British Empire.

EUROPEANS EXPLORE THE AFRICAN INTERIOR

European nations had explored much of the coastline of Africa, establishing trading outposts and implementing the slave trade. Its vast interior, however, still lay largely untouched by Europeans until explorers and missionaries ventured further inland in the late eighteenth and nineteenth centuries.

Two Scots explorers were among the first Europeans to explore the interior: James Bruce, on his travels to Abyssinia (Ethiopia), found the source of the Blue Nile, and in 1795, Mungo Park explored the Gambia and was reportedly the first Westerner to reach the River Niger. In the following century, the Paris-based Société de Géographie offered a 10,000-franc prize to the first non-Muslim who returned with information on Timbuktu – the prize was claimed in 1828 by Frenchman René Caillé after his safe return from the

West African town. By 1835, most of north-western Africa had been mapped by Europeans.

From the mid-nineteenth century, the most famous of all European explorers was the Scottish Protestant missionary David Livingstone who discovered and renamed Victoria Falls (in honour of the British monarch Queen Victoria) in 1855. In 1866 he led an expedition in search of the Nile, his mysterious disappearance and death further sparking obsession with the African interior. In 1858, the British explorers John Hanning Speke and Sir Richard Burton became the first Europeans to reach Lake Tanganyika. Speke also went on to reach another great lake which he renamed, not unsurprisingly, Lake Victoria (and which eventually proved to be the source of the Nile). In 1875, the British traveller Verney Cameron was the first European to cross the continent from east to west.

The Slave Trade and Abolition

The transportation of slaves from Africa to the European colonies in the Americas increased dramatically during the eighteenth century. In the 1780s, 90,000 African slaves were transported across the Atlantic each year, and by the mid-nineteenth century an estimated 9.5 million Africans had been transported to the New World, representing the largest forced migration in history.

The Atlantic slave trade usually followed a triangular system in which ships from Europe sailed to West Africa carrying cotton goods, hardware, and weaponry (the West Africans used these firearms to capture slaves). These goods were exchanged for slaves who were taken to the Americas, and the ships then returned to Europe with sugar and other colonial produce.

In addition to the 9.5 million slaves transported, around 2 million slaves died in transit. In Europe, awareness of the brutal realities of slavery grew and in the late eighteenth century religious groups in Britain began to campaign for its abolition. In 1807, Britain (the chief trading nation) made the trade illegal for British merchants, although the transportation of slaves – particularly to North America, Brazil and Cuba where demand for cotton and sugar was high – continued unabated. West African rulers, whose economies were heavily dependent on slavery, were also reluctant to stop capturing and selling slaves. Slavery itself wasn't abolished in the British Empire until 1833.

The abolition of slavery in the United States in 1865 during the American Civil War (see page 140) eventually forced Cuba and Brazil to follow suit in 1886 and 1888. While this spelled the end of the Atlantic slave trade, Arab and African merchants still transported slaves to North and East Africa, a practice that didn't finally come to end until the twentieth century.

THE SCRAMBLE FOR AFRICA

Europe's exploration of the interior of Africa (see page 112), along with new information about its untapped resources of minerals, precious metals and tropical raw goods, heightened the interest of European powers whose industries were crying out for raw materials. This, combined with a heightened tension on the political map of Europe, led to a frenzied partitioning of Africa in the last quarter of the nineteenth century (called the 'Scramble for Africa' after an 1884 conference in Berlin which encouraged European rivals to divide up the continent).

Wars raged across west, central and eastern Africa as Europeans fought among themselves and against African nations. France secured territories in much of the north, west and around the equator; the Germans and Belgians gained colonies along the Congo; and in the south, the Portuguese occupied Angola and Mozambique, while Britain dominated the east from South Africa to Egypt, as well as parts of the west (amounting to over 4 million square miles or 10.3 million square km of land). Other European nations – including the Italians and Spanish – claimed what remained.

Many African nations and rulers – including the Ashanti, Abyssinians, the Dervishes, Zulus and Moroccans – fought against this wave of European aggression, initially with some success, but most were powerless in the face of the Europeans' superior firepower. European overlords drew up boundaries of colonies without any reference to local geography, tribal distribution and language. By 1914, only Ethiopia and Liberia remained independent states: Ethiopia (formerly Abyssinia) successfully fought off Italian colonization in 1896, while Liberia had been established as an independent state for liberated American slaves in the first half of the nineteenth century.

SOUTHERN AFRICA

Since 1652, the coastal region of South Africa had been colonized by the Dutch (known as the Boer or Afrikaners). The region's indigenous population, the San and Khoikhoin, were either forced into subjugation or displaced (the San withdrew into the mountains). In the 1770s the Boers moved inland where they encountered the more settled Xhosa people. There followed a century of wars (the Xhosa Wars, 1779–1879) as Dutch and British colonists pushed further east into the Great Fish River region.

To protect the sea route to India, Britain had taken over the Cape of Good Hope area in 1795, and finally colonized the Cape Colony in 1806. In a bid to escape British control in the Cape (and its abolition of slavery), 12,000 Boers moved northwards between 1835–43 in the Great Trek. They migrated to the future Natal, Orange Free State and Transvaal regions. Initially, Britain recognized their independence.

In the meantime, the Zulus (a warlike Bantu-speaking people) had grown in power and expanded their territory under their leader, Shaka (ruled 1816–28), which led to widespread warfare amongst indigenous tribes between around 1815 and 1840. In 1879, the British invaded the Zulu kingdom and after a defeat at Isandhlwana, captured the capital. Zululand was made a British colony in 1887 and ten years later incorporated into Natal.

The discovery of gold and diamonds in the Transvaal region led to attempts by the British (secretly supported by the imperialist Cecil Rhodes) to take over the Transvaal. London had become the financial hub of the world and needed a constant flow of gold to supply it. This eventually led to a bitter three-year struggle between the Boers and the British between 1899 and 1902. The Boers secured some initial victories but were finally defeated by British reinforcements and Kitchener's 'scorched-earth' policies of systematically destroying farms and interring the civil population in concentration camps. The peace treaty of 1902 recognized British rule and led to a union of all South African territories in 1910.

Nadir Shah Rules Persia

Often described as the 'Napoleon of Persia', Nadir Shah, who ruled Persia from 1736 to 1747, led a series of impressive military campaigns to create an empire that briefly encompassed present-day Iran, Iraq, Afghanistan, Pakistan, Oman, and parts of central Asia and the Caucasus region.

Of Turkish origin, Nadir grew up in northern Persia during the final years of the Safavid dynasty (see pages 83–4), coming to prominence during a period of anarchy in Persia after the weak Safavid Shah Sultan Husayn had been overthrown by Hotaki Afghans, and the Ottomans and Russians had invaded. Nadir raised an army of 5,000 to help Husayn's son Shah Tahmasp II regain the throne, whilst also repelling the Ottomans and Russians and regaining any Persian territory lost to them. By 1736, Nadir himself seized the throne and proclaimed himself shah.

Thereon Nadir embarked upon expeditions against neighbouring states, conquering Afghanistan, and invading the Mughal Empire in India. There, he captured Kabul,

Lahore and Peshawar and sacked Delhi in 1739, killing around 30,000 and looting huge amounts of treasure, including the Mughal's fabled peacock throne and Koh-i-noor diamond (which eventually became part of the British crown jewels).

Thereafter, Nadir's health declined and his rule became increasingly despotic. In 1747 he was eventually assassinated by one of his own guards, and his empire quickly disintegrated. One of his generals, however, Ahmad Shah, took over Nadir's Afghan provinces and conquests in north-west India until his death in 1773.

FAR EAST

THE APOGEE OF MANCHU CHINA

China's last imperial dynasty, the Manchu (founders of the Qing dynasty from 1644–1911), encountered some opposition in its early years, but from around 1683, it secured control over the whole of China and thereon enjoyed a century-long period of peace and prosperity, often known as 'Pax Sinica' (Peace in China).

Qing rule differed little from previous dynasties although officials were made to wear pigtails (a Manchu custom) as a sign of loyalty. The Qing promoted Confucian scholarship and the Confucian basis of society, although Jesuit missionaries were allowed into the empire, converting around 200,000 to Christianity during the reign of Emperor Kangxi (1661–1722 – the longest reign of any Chinese emperor).

China reached the peak of its power during the reign of Kangxi's grandson, Qianlong (1735–96). Agricultural and industrial advances increased the wealth of the empire, as did increased trade with Europe. The arts and learning were also encouraged: Qianlong sponsored huge volumes of literary classics; and architecture, porcelain, painting and jade and ivory work flourished.

The Qing dynasty also saw the territory of China increase three-fold, with the incorporation of Taiwan, Manchuria, Mongolia, Tibet and Turkistan. The population grew quickly from 100 million to 300 million by the end of the eighteenth century, which led to a shortage of land and the onset of rebellion, as corruption again spread within the imperial court. Throughout the nineteenth century, the Qing increasingly proved unable to cope with major internal revolts, most notably the Taiping Rebellion (see page 121), as well as mounting intrusion from Western powers (see pages 121–2, 150).

THE BRITISH IN INDIA

Nadir Shah's invasion of India (see pages 117–18) had exposed the weakness of the Mughal emperors, whose power had increasingly fallen into the hands of provincial viceroys. By 1700 the British East India Company, having moved its attention towards India, had established important trading ports in Madras, Bombay and Calcutta.

By the mid-1700s Anglo–French hostility in Europe had led to a struggle of supremacy between the British and French in India. The British general and colonial administrator Robert Clive ('Clive of India') succeeded in outmanoeuvring the French in south India (after French forces had taken the

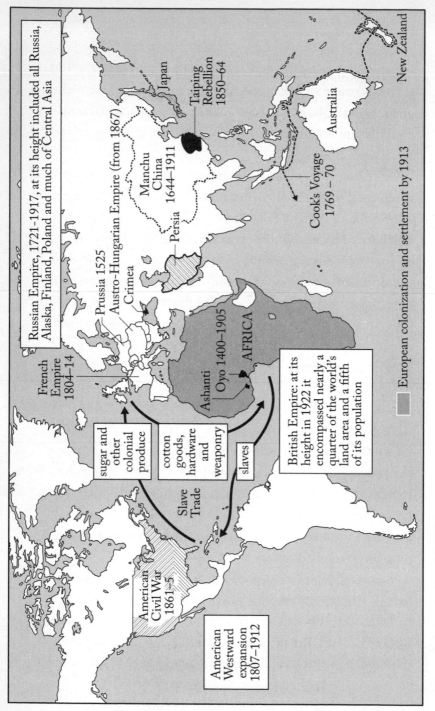

Russian Empire, 1721-1917, at its height included all Russia,
Alaska, Finland, Poland and much of Central Asia

New Zealand

Japan

Taiping
Rebellion
1850-64

Austro-Hungarian Empire (from 1867)

Manchu
China
1644-1911

Persia

Australia

Cook's Voyage
1769 - 70

Prussia 1525

Crimea

European colonization and settlement by 1913

French
Empire
1804-14

Ashanti
Oyo 1400-1905   AFRICA

sugar and
other
colonial
produce

cotton
goods,
hardware
and
weaponry

British Empire: at its
height in 1922 it
encompassed nearly a
quarter of the world's
land area and a fifth
of its population

slaves

Slave
Trade

American Civil War
1861-5

American
Westward
expansion
1807-1912

5   Expansion up to the First World War 1400-1911

city of Madras). In 1757, he recaptured Calcutta from Nawab (Nabob) Siraj ud daula and his victory at Plassey later that year brought Bengal, India's richest province with 20 million inhabitants, under the control of the East India Company.

Over the next few decades, the British steadily expanded their influence over the region, though with strong French competition, so that by 1806 the whole of India was under either direct control or at least the influence of the East India Company. The company also kept an army of 300,000, the most formidable in Asia, which helped to keep control in India (and which also fought extensively abroad).

As the Industrial Revolution took hold in Britain, India increasingly exported raw materials (such as indigo and raw cotton, as well as opium to China) rather than finished cloth. In tandem, the East India Company acted more as an instrument of colonial government, having lost its monopoly of trade with India in 1813. Widespread uprisings in 1857 during the Indian Mutiny led to control of India passing from the East India Company to the British government in 1858, with Queen Victoria proclaimed as Empress of India in 1876.

THE OPIUM WARS AND TAIPING REBELLION IN CHINA

As the Qing (Manchu) dynasty weakened in authority, China became increasingly vulnerable to foreign intervention, while civil war and rebellion devastated its economy and led to the loss of millions of lives.

In the early nineteenth century, British traders, intent on

opening up trade in China, were illegally exporting opium from India to China in exchange for Chinese tea and silks. Opium was popular among the British elite and helped against dysentery, which was common in China. To prevent the trade, the Chinese seized and destroyed over 20,000 chests of opium and 42,000 pipes from British warehouses. The British then sent a force of sixteen British warships, which besieged Canton (Guangzhou) and in 1842, captured Shanghai. The war ended with the Treaty of Nanjing in which Hong Kong was ceded to the British.

The Second Opium War (1856-60) broke out when the Qing authorities refused to renegotiate more favourable terms for the Nanjing Treaty. This time the French joined the British in launching an attack: Beijing was overthrown and the Chinese agreed to the Treaty of Tianjin in 1860, which opened another ten ports to Western trade.

At the same time, the Manchu faced a major series of peasant risings, brought on in part by the Qing's corrupt administration and China's rising population (by 1850 the Chinese population stood at 450 million). This culminated in civil war in 1850 when the religious fanatic Hong Xiuquan, intent on freeing China from Manchu rule, led a rebel army one-million strong towards Nanjing. The rebels captured Nanjing in 1853, established the 'Taiping Heavenly Kingdom', then the revolt spread to another fifteen provinces. With the help of British and French forces, Nanjing was recaptured in 1864 and the rebellion was eventually put down. The war had cost some 20 million lives, both civilian and military (representing the most destructive civil war in history); whole towns and villages were destroyed, and the Qing dynasty never recovered its authority or status.

THE MEIJI RESTORATION IN JAPAN

Since 1639, Japan had had little contact with the outside world due to the isolationist foreign policy of the Tokugawa shōgunate (see page 86), which severely limited foreign trade and forbade any Japanese to leave or foreigner to enter the country. This ended in 1853 when four US naval ships arrived and compelled Japan to open two ports to US trade.

Further treaties with other powers, including Britain and Russia, followed, concessions for which signalled the weakness of the shōgunate. By 1866 there was open rebellion by *daimyō* (landowners or magnates), which led to the resignation of the last Tokugawa shōgun and the restoration of imperial rule under the Meiji Emperor Mutsuhito in 1868. The slogan of the Meiji was 'wealthy country and strong arms'.

A year later, the imperial capital was moved from Kyōto to Edo (and renamed Tokyo) and a series of reforms, designed to strengthen and modernize Japan so that it could resist Western domination, were put in place. A Western-style constitution was introduced and the *daimyō* and samurai system dismantled. A national educational system was established (giving Japan an almost 100 per cent literacy rate by 1900) and foreign advice was sought on matters of agriculture, finance, engineering and military technology. Government-sponsored industrial development was implemented with the establishment of factories, dockyards and the railway, and exports soared from 30 million yen in 1878–82 to 932 million yen in 1913–17.

Japan's modernization enabled her to defeat China in the Sino–Japanese War (1894–95), which was fought between China and Japan over the control of Korea. The Chinese were forced to accept Korean independence and cede territories to Japan, including Taiwan. Japan also shocked Europe when she destroyed Russian troops, both on land and sea, in the Russo–Japanese War (1904–5), which led to a shift of power balance in the East, and the Russian Revolution of 1905 (see pages 163–4).

EUROPE

THE RISE OF RUSSIA

In the eighteenth century, Russia emerged as an important power in Europe. Over the previous two centuries, it had grown from the small principality of Muscovy to an empire that stretched 7,500 miles (12,000 km) from the Baltic Sea to the Pacific Ocean.

While large, Russia was still relatively isolated and less developed than the rest of Europe. Peter I (the Great) – who ruled with his half-brother Ivan V from 1682–96, and as sole ruler until 1725 – took measures to transform Russia into a partially Westernized empire. Intent on building a great Baltic seaport, marshes were drained near the River Neva to create St Petersburg (Peter's 'window on the West'). The tsar replaced old systems of government in line with Western Europe, promoted education, reorganized the Church and even outlawed among the ruling classes the wearing of traditional long kaftans and long hair or beards.

Having modernized his armed forces (and built Russia's first navy), Peter then waged the Great Northern War against Sweden, which, following the victories of Gustavus Adolphus in the Thirty Years War, had become the greatest power in northern Europe. Russia's eventually victory in 1721 gave Peter access to the Baltic Sea and he went on to annex Estonia, Latvia and parts of Finland. (Less successful was Peter's attack on the Ottoman Empire in 1710 after which he was forced to return the Black Sea ports he had seized in 1697.)

After Peter the Great's death in 1725, Russian territory and influence continued to grow. Under the empresses Elizabeth I and Catherine the Great, Russia came to dominate Poland and won a series of victories against the Ottoman Turks. By 1815, following the final defeat of Napoleon (see page 130), Russia and Austria were confirmed as the leading powers in Continental Europe.

The Wars of the 1700s and the Emergence of Prussia

The beginning of the eighteenth century saw much of Europe involved in conflict over control of Spain and its empire. The Wars of Spanish Succession (1702–13) arose when the French prince Philip of Anjou was made heir to the Spanish throne. The prospect of a union between Spain and France sent shockwaves throughout Europe, and an alliance was formed in 1701 between the British, the Dutch and most of the German princes in support of an Austrian claim to the

Spanish Empire. Fighting took place mainly in Europe, but also in North America where the English fought the French in 'Queen Anne's War' between 1702 and 1713. The wars ended with the Treaty of Utrecht in 1713, which recognized Philip of Anjou as Philip V of Spain, but removed him from the French line of succession, whilst in North America, Britain gained considerable territory.

In the meantime, the kingdom of Prussia (proclaimed in 1701), with its large standing army, emerged as a serious rival to Austria for supremacy in Germany. In 1740, Frederick the Great of Prussia seized the rich Austrian province of Silesia, and held on to it during eight years of war (in the War of the Austrian Succession). The struggle was renewed in the Seven Years War (1756–63), during which Prussia fought against Russia, France, Austria and Sweden, while her ally Britain clashed with France in North America, Africa and India. The war concluded with no significant changes to the European map, although Silesia remained Prussian and Prussia clearly stood among the ranks of great powers. Great Britain gained the bulk of New France (Canada and America east of the Mississippi), Spanish Florida, Senegal and superiority over French outposts in India. Britain was now firmly established as a leading colonial power and it had been consolidated internally too by the union with Scotland in 1707.

THE AGE OF ENLIGHTENMENT
The Enlightenment, or Age of Reason, was a cultural and philosophical movement underpinned by a belief in the power of reason. It was influenced by the development of scientific

knowledge in the seventeenth century, notably by the French rationalist philosopher and mathematician René Descartes (1596–1650), and later by the English mathematician Isaac Newton (1642–1727) whose insights into the laws of gravity and motion influenced the work of many other scientists across Europe.

Gaining momentum in the eighteenth century, Enlightenment thinkers questioned established institutions and the accepted social order and attacked both superstition and the Church itself as an enemy of reason. Writers and philosophers, such as Voltaire and Rousseau in France, began to apply Enlightenment principles to society, making the case that all people are equal. In Britain, Adam Smith and David Hume advocated economic liberalism and empiricism, and the political writer Thomas Paine wrote in support of American independence and the French Revolution.

The intellectual force of the Enlightenment spread to other urban centres in Europe, and powerful European rulers welcomed philosophers into their courts (but did not always carry out their progressive ideas when it did not suit them). Frederick the Great of Prussia patronized philosophers and scientists and saw himself as a leader of the Enlightenment, whilst in Russia the government, particularly under Catherine the Great, actively encouraged the proliferation of the arts and sciences. In North America, its ideals influenced Benjamin Franklin and Thomas Jefferson, two of the founding fathers of the United States.

Aided by the widespread distribution of the printing press, the theories of the Enlightenment influenced politics, law, economics, scientific theory and the arts, and formed the intellectual basis for the French and American Revolutions (see below and page 136).

THE FRENCH REVOLUTION

Pre-revolutionary France epitomized Old Europe: its kings Louis XV and XVI, the Sun King's successors, failed to reform convincingly enough and continued to live in ostentatious splendour. They, along with the aristocracy, were entirely exempt from paying tax, whereas the middle class and the poor were forced to sustain the country in peace and war. France's involvement in costly wars eventually led to financial crisis, while bad harvests in the 1780s brought high food prices and crippling poverty to much of the population.

In 1789, to deal with the crisis, the government met with the so-called Estates General, a representative assembly made up of the nobility, clergy and the middle classes (the Third Estate). When it became clear that the nobility and clergy could over-rule the third estate, its bourgeois leaders began a struggle for equal rights by reconvening and declaring itself the National Assembly. In Paris an angry mob stormed the Bastille on 14 July 1789, and a series of peasant rebellions spread throughout much of France. The National Assembly then abolished noble privileges, produced a Declaration of the Rights of Man and attempted to establish the principles of equality, citizenship and inalienable rights.

Increasing military threats from Austria and Prussia led to more radical policies: the monarchy was abolished and a republic established in 1792, and King Louis XVI and Queen

Marie Antoinette were executed in 1793. Thereon an extreme wing of the government, the Committee of Public Safety, led by the 'Jacobins' and their leader Maximilien Robespierre rose to power, unleashing a 'Reign of Terror' in which around 40,000 people – many of them peasants or urban workers – were executed. When Robespierre himself was sent to the guillotine in 1794, the Terror ended. In 1795, the Directory assumed control of the French state until the young general Napoleon Bonaparte (see below) seized power in 1799.

THE FRENCH REVOLUTIONARY AND NAPOLEONIC WARS AND VIENNA SETTLEMENT

Between 1792 and 1815 various European coalitions fought against the French; first in the French Revolutionary Wars (1792–1802) in which France sought to defend and spread republicanism; then in the Napoleonic Wars (1803–15) in which Napoleon Bonaparte sought to dominate Europe.

Austria, Prussia, Spain, the United Provinces and Britain formed the first coalition against France, initially with the intention to restore Louis XVI to power. By 1796, France's new commander Napoleon Bonaparte secured a series of decisive victories against the Austrians in northern Italy, and by early 1797, France had broken up the coalition and isolated Britain. In 1798, however, Napoleon was defeated by Admiral Horatio Nelson in Egypt at the Battle of the Nile. A year later, Napoleon defeated the Austrians at Marengo and peace treaties with Austria (1801) and Britain (1802) ended the Revolutionary Wars.

In 1803, war erupted again, and in 1805, Nelson destroyed

the combined Spanish and French fleet at the Battle of Trafalgar, during which he was mortally wounded. In the same year, Napoleon defeated Austria and Russia at the Battle of Austerlitz. Much of Western Europe now lay under the control of the French Empire. Napoleon next set his sights on Spain but was repelled from the Iberian Peninsula in 1811 by Spain, Portugal and Britain. Napoleon was finally crushed when he attacked Russia in 1812 – up to half a million of his men perished during its bitter winter. In 1814, Napoleon was forced to abdicate; he briefly retook power in 1815 but was defeated by Prussian, British and Belgian forces at Waterloo.

The ensuing Congress of Vienna, masterminded by the Austrian statesman Prince von Metternich in 1814–15, established a new balance of power in Europe centred on the five 'Great Powers': Britain, France, Prussia, Austria and Russia. The political map of Europe was redrawn, with a new king reinstated in France, republican Holland reunited with Belgium under one king, and Poland and Italy redistributed among the Great Powers. The settlement is credited by some historians with preventing widespread European war for nearly a century.

THE INDUSTRIAL REVOLUTION

During the eighteenth century, improved farming methods in Britain, along with large-scale enclosure of farmland, boosted agricultural output. This supported population growth and the rise of a new class of landless labourer, all of which helped drive forward a major transition in Britain's manufacturing, known as the Industrial Revolution.

Key developments in the industrial revolution included the introduction of machinery into the textile industry (such as James Hargreaves's Spinning Jenny, patented in 1770); Richard Arkwright's first factory in 1771; the mass-production of pig iron from blast furnaces fuelled by coke, rather than charcoal (developed by Abraham Darby in 1709); and the use of steam-powered engines that could run factory machines (as developed by Scottish engineer James Watt in 1782). These technical advances facilitated the rise of large-scale factories based on mechanized labour over that of rural, manual labour or the manufacture of products at home (the cottage industry). Industrialization also sped up urbanization and by 1850, half of the British population lived in cities.

Industrialization also went hand in hand with improvements in transport: thousands of new roads were built in Britain in the 1700s, along with a vast network of canals. In 1825, the world's first passenger steam railway was built using George Stephenson's *Rocket* steam locomotive, and by 1855, thousands of railway tracks snaked across Britain.

The process of industrialization spread to Europe in the nineteenth century. New coalfields in the Ruhr and Pas de Calais facilitated the expansion of the railway from the 1850s, and after unification in 1871, industry spread rapidly in Germany, particularly in the steel, chemicals and electrical industries. Railways were built across Europe and the world, with the US completing the first transcontinental railroad in 1869. (In fact industrialization increased exponentially in the US so that by 1900 it was a leading industrial power.)

INDUSTRIAL SOCIETY, MARXISM AND REVOLT

Whilst industrialists and middle-class businessmen thrived during the Industrial Revolution, life for the ordinary worker was still harsh and unrelenting.

The concentration of working people in mills, factories and urban areas led to a sense of solidarity, and also to the emergence of trade unions to help advance their interests. The first real working-class movement in Britain was the Chartists, who from 1838 agitated for the universal vote. (The 1832 Reform Act had extended the vote in Britain but did not grant anything like universal suffrage.) But by 1848 the Chartist movement had disintegrated, partly through governmental repression and partly through lack of momentum.

On the continent of Europe, discontent and unemployment among the working classes, an upsurge in nationalism, and rising demands by liberal middle classes for constitutional and social reform, led to a series of revolts during 1848. The revolutionary wave began in France and spread to much of Europe, including Hungary, Austria, Ireland, Switzerland, Denmark, and many German and Italian states. By the end of 1849, all the revolts had been quashed but the governments had been forced to listen to the voice of the people and the ideals of democracy, liberalism, nationalism and socialism had gained in popularity.

Two writers who gave voice to the politics of the working class were the Germans Karl Marx and Friedrich Engels. Setting out their ideas in the *Communist Manifesto*, published in 1848, they believed that economic forces shaped all history and that a socialist state – that is, a classless society based on common ownership and production – could only be achieved through violent revolution. This alarmed the middle-class liberals of Europe – many of whom admired the parliamentary government of Britain – who chose to work within the old regimes provided they were given a voice in government.

'THE EASTERN QUESTION' AND THE CRIMEAN WAR

'The Eastern Question' arose as the power of the Ottoman Empire began to decline, in particular after the Russo–Turkish War (1768–74), which ended in defeat for the Ottomans. Thereafter, the Great Powers of Europe engaged in a power struggle to safeguard their interest in Ottoman territory, believing the collapse of the Ottoman Empire was imminent.

Russia, eager to have access to the Mediterranean and to control the Black Sea, stood to benefit most from the collapse of the Ottoman Empire; whilst Austria and Britain, in a bid to contain Russian expansion, sought to maintain the unity of the empire. The Eastern Question arose again in the nineteenth century when the Greeks finally won independence from the Ottoman Turks in 1832. This signalled the further weakening of the Ottomans, whose empire continued to exist largely because rival European powers supported it.

The Crimean War (1853–6), fought by Russia against the Allied forces of Turkey, Britain, France and Piedmont, was largely caused by this long-running rivalry, and was triggered when Russian forces attacked a Turkish fleet.

Most of the conflict took place on the Crimean peninsula and resulted in heavy loss of life: a third of the 1.2 million soldiers who fought died, including a disproportionate number due to disease. Allied troops were ill equipped and badly prepared, although hospital conditions improved with the intervention of Florence Nightingale and Mary Seacole and their pioneering work on hygiene standards. The Allies eventually won, with Russia signing a peace treaty in 1856, forcing her to remove her naval fleets from the Black Sea.

POPULATION MIGRATIONS

The growth in European empires also led to large-scale emigration from Europe, particularly in the nineteenth century when Europe's population more than doubled. In the 1830s, European emigration overseas for the first time passed the figure of 100,000 a year, and between 1840 and 1930 it's thought that around 50 million people left Europe to go overseas.

The vast majority of European emigrants went to North America (many of them British, German and Irish). Between 1800 and 1917, around 36 million Europeans left for the US; 6 million Europeans went to South America, particularly to Argentina and Brazil where Spanish, Italians, Portuguese and Germans settled; and another 5 million (mainly British and French) went to Canada.

Many emigrants sought better lives, plentiful and cheap land, and employment. Some, however, went against their will: British convicts were sent to Australia (see page 142), French convicts to New Caledonia and French Guiana; while

Russian Jews left to escape persecution (to central Asia or the Balkans).

Between 1845–51, a million people lost their lives during the Irish famine, and another million left the country. The majority of Irish emigrants went to North America: by 1850, the Irish made up a quarter of the population in many of the US's cities, while thousands also emigrated to Canada and Australia as well as England and Scotland. While Europe's population grew, Ireland's plummeted from 5.5 million in 1871 to 4.4 million in 1911. The famine, caused by potato blight, was the last great subsistence crisis of Europe, affecting not just Ireland but other areas in northern Europe.

THE RISE OF THE NATION STATE

Nationalism – the idea that groups of people united by race, language or history should rule their own country – evolved into a powerful political force in nineteenth-century Europe. The Congress of Vienna (see page 130), in its concern for a balance of power in Europe, had largely disregarded national impulses.

Nationalism generally triumphed when it was supported by a major power in Europe: Belgium secured independence from Holland in 1830, with the help of France and Britain; Greece broke away from the Ottoman Empire in 1832 because it was aided by the Great Powers of Europe; and later in the century, the Serbs, Bulgars, Romanian and Armenians all established nation states.

Similarly, in Italy, the statesman Count Cavour succeeded in driving the Austrians from Italy with the help of Napoleon

III of France, and by 1870, following Giuseppe Garibaldi's victory in Sicily and Southern Italy, all of Italy was united.

In Germany, the Austro–Prussian War of 1866 had led to Prussian dominance over German states, and an impetus towards German unification without Austria. The defeat was a telling blow for the Austrian Empire, which had been weakened by nationalist revolts: the former Austrian province of Venetia was handed to France, then Italy (Prussia's ally), and in 1867 the Austro-Hungarian Compromise created the autonomous states of Hungary and Austria under the Austrian emperor. (This diverse rule increasingly came under pressure from various subject nations, such as the Serbs, Croats, Czechs and Poles. Failure to resolve these nationalist aspirations was one of the causes of the First World War.)

The Franco–Prussian War (1870–1) led to defeat for France (and the loss of Alsace and Lorraine to the Germans). On a tide of German nationalist excitement and a measure of compromise, the German states in 1871 proclaimed their union under their new emperor William I, with the statesman Bismarck as his chancellor. The new empire of Germany swiftly become the dominant power in continental Europe.

THE AMERICAS

The American Revolution
During the eighteenth century, relations between Britain and its American colonies deteriorated, caused largely by colonial resentment over their lack of representation in the British Parliament. Tension grew when Britain attempted to raise

new taxes, which culminated in a series of protests including the Boston Tea Party in 1773, when colonists dumped three shiploads of tea into the Boston harbour.

Armed resistance led to full-scale war in 1776, after King George III refused to compromise over taxes or listen to the colonists' grievances. Public sentiment increasingly favoured independence – fuelled in part by the liberal and democratic ideals of the Enlightenment and the publication of Thomas Paine's incendiary pamphlet 'Common Sense' (which argued for freedom from British rule).

With no hope of a peaceful outcome, on 4 July 1776 the colonists adopted the Declaration of Independence, which unified the American colonies as 'free and independent states ... absolved from all Allegiance to the British crown'. The fighting continued for another five years: British troops suffered from lack of supplies and local knowledge, and despite frequent victories, could not destroy George Washington's armies or the American will.

A French alliance with the Continental Congress in 1778 also changed the nature of the war – particularly as Britain was distracted by war in Europe and the West and East Indies – and it was a Franco-American force that won the final major battle at Yorktown, Virginia, in 1781. The 1783 Treaty of Paris finally recognized the independence of the United States of America. In 1787, representatives of the American colonies drew up a remarkably advanced federal constitution that provided the framework for representative democracy in the United States.

SPANISH-AMERICAN WARS OF INDEPENDENCE

The revolutions of North America and France, along with the liberal ideas of the Enlightenment, also inspired the Spanish colonies in the Americas to fight for independence. From around 1808 to 1825 independence was established throughout South and Central America with Spain no longer controlling any part of the continent other than the Caribbean islands of Cuba and Puerto Rico (which remained under Spanish rule until 1898).

The trigger for conflict arose in 1808 when the Spanish monarchy was deposed by Napoleon's brother Joseph during the Peninsular War. The French occupation destroyed the Spanish administration, which fragmented into provincial juntas and general confusion. Many of the Spanish colonies considered themselves able to appoint their own juntas, which ultimately led to conflict between patriots who promoted autonomy and the royalists who believed Spain still had authority.

Two of the most important leaders in the fight for independence were the patriots Simón Bolívar and José de San Martin. In 1813 Bolívar led a revolt in Venezuela and established its independence by 1821. He then carried the struggle to Colombia, defeated the Spanish and became its first president. He subsequently linked up with the independence movement in the south under the leadership of José de San Martin. San Martin, with his second-in-command Bernardo O'Higgins (who was half-Irish, half-Chilean), had defeated the royalist armies and enabled Chile to declare independence in 1818 (where O'Higgins became its dictator and ruled for five years).

Both movements then closed in on the Spanish stronghold of Lima, Peru. Peruvian independence was declared in 1821 and San Martin became its Protector for a year. The independence of Argentina was declared in 1816, Mexico in 1821, and the Portuguese colony of Brazil was declared independent by Dom Pedro I in 1822.

North American Expansion and 'Manifest Destiny'

During the nineteenth century, the United States established itself further into the North American continent, pushing west towards the Pacific coast 'from sea to shining sea'. In 1803, the purchase of the Louisiana territories from the French virtually doubled the size of the United States; in 1820 Florida, Missouri and Maine were added to the Union; and by 1848 Texas, California and New Mexico were included following war with Mexico (1846–8).

Meanwhile, in 1846, the Oregon Treaty with Britain led to US ownership of the north-west Pacific area while the Californian Gold Rush of 1849 brought an influx of hundreds of thousands of gold-seekers (known as the 'forty-niners'). Between 1860 and 1900 millions of Americans and European immigrants settled on these new lands and by the end of the Spanish–American War in 1898, the Union had purchased Alaska from the Russians, annexed Hawaii and taken control of a number of overseas territories, including Puerto Rico, Guam and the Philippines.

The doctrine of 'manifest destiny' played a significant

part in raising support for US expansionism. It was a phrase first coined by the *New York Morning News* editor John O'Sullivan in 1845 to urge the annexation of Texas. Manifest destiny evolved into a moral ideology, one that presented expansionism as a divine mission, and which consequently sanctioned the forced removal of Native Americans from their land (along with the massacre of millions of buffalo).

Facing homelessness and starvation, Native Americans fought back, most famously at the Battle of Little Bighorn in 1876 when Sioux and Cheyenne warriors killed 268 US soldiers under Lieutenant-Colonel Custer (an action known as 'Custer's Last Stand'). US forces clamped down on further resistance, finally defeating the Native Americans at the Wounded Knee massacre in 1890. Surviving Native Americans – approximately 500,000 as compared to the 4.5 million who had inhabited North America in 1500 – were confined to reservations (relatively small areas given to them by the US government).

THE AMERICAN CIVIL WAR

As America pursued its policy of expansion, tensions mounted between the industrialized states of the north, which had for the most part abandoned slavery, and the agricultural, slave-owning states in the south. When Abraham Lincoln, the candidate of the anti-slavery Republican Party, was elected president in 1860, the Southern states, fearing that Lincoln would attempt to abolish slavery, split from the Union to form a Confederacy. The South's principal aim was to be recognized as an independent nation, whereas Lincoln's primary motive at the outset of war was to preserve the Union.

Fighting began in 1861 when Confederate troops opened fire on Union forces at Fort Sumter in South Carolina. Both sides quickly began raising armies: and on 21 July some 30,000 Union forces were driven back from Manassas in Virginia by Confederate forces led by General 'Stonewall' Jackson and General Beauregard. The defeat shocked the Union, which quickly called for 500,000 more soldiers. In 1863, Lincoln issued the Emancipation Proclamation (which promised freedom for slaves held in any Confederate states that did not return to the Union by end of the year). This gave a new moral aim to the war, now that conciliation with the South proved untenable.

In 1863, the Union gained control of the Mississippi River at the Battle of Vicksburg. At the same time, Union forces drove out attacking Confederate troops at the Battle of Gettysburg, halting the Confederates' advance north. (Lincoln gave his famous Gettysburg Address on the site in November 1863.) Gradually the South was worn down as Union general William Sherman captured Atlanta and Savannah, Georgia. The supreme commander of the Union forces, General Ulysses S. Grant, began his final advance in April 1865 and on 9 April received Confederate leader, Robert E. Lee's surrender at Appomattox. Victory for the North resulted in the abolition of slavery in the US, the end of the Confederacy and a strengthening of federal government. It was also one of the most brutal wars in US history, with over 600,000 Americans killed, more than in any war before or since.

OCEANIA

Captain James Cook and European Settlement of Australia

Between 1768 and 1779, British naval captain and navigator James Cook led three expeditions into the Pacific, during which he reached Tahiti and every major South Pacific island group; sailed around New Zealand and landed on the east coast of Australia (which he claimed for Britain, naming it New South Wales); and discovered and explored Hawaii (where he was killed in 1779). His detailed accounts contributed much to European knowledge of Oceania, and also initiated extensive colonization by European settlers.

In 1788, eighteen years after Captain Cook's first landing, a fleet of British ships – containing 759 convicts – arrived at Botany Bay, Australia, before establishing a settlement at Sydney Cove. Over the next eighty years, over 160,000 convicts were sent to the penal settlements of New South Wales, Van Dieman's Land (Tasmania – settled in 1803) and Western Australia (founded in 1829). Convicts formed the majority of the colonies' population in the first few decades, although voluntary settlers began to arrive from the 1820s onwards. Separate colonies were formed out of New South Wales to become South Australia in 1836, Victoria in 1851 and Queensland in 1859. The indigenous Aborigine population estimated at 750,000 to a million, declined steeply for 150 years after settlement, mainly due to infectious diseases (such as smallpox). Squatter settlements, particularly in eastern Australia, also led to violent conflict with the Aborigines.

Gold rushes in the 1850s and 1860s led to a large influx of immigrants and increased government spending on infrastructure. Transportation of convicts ended in 1868 when the population had grown to 1 million and the colonies were able to support themselves without the need for convicts. Towards the end of the century, each of Australia's six colonies began to explore the prospect for federation as a nation.

EUROPEAN COLONIZATION OF NEW ZEALAND AND THE PACIFIC ISLANDS

After Captain Cook had mapped the coastline of New Zealand in 1769 (see previous page), foreign ships began arriving on its shores, first setting up stations for seal and whale hunting and later establishing farms, mines and permanent settlements. A variety of goods were traded, often in exchange for the musket, which the indigenous Maori used to devastating effect in their inter-tribal wars (1801–40), in which 30–40,000 Maori (out of a population of 150,000) died. New infectious diseases brought by the settlers also led to further Maori decline.

In 1840, Britain formally annexed New Zealand, and the number of immigrants began to increase. Conflict over land ownership led to the New Zealand Wars of the 1860s and 1870s, which resulted in the loss and confiscation of much Maori land. Three gold rushes in the 1860s led to a huge increase in the white population, to 248,000, while the Maori population dwindled to 38,500. In 1852, New Zealand was granted home rule and its own Parliament (General Assembly) and in 1907 became a self-governing dominion.

Other islands in the Pacific were also subject to extensive colonization, including Tahiti, which was annexed by France in 1880; Tonga, whose ruling Tu'i Kanokupolu dynasty united into a more Westernized kingdom in 1845, before becoming a British-protected state in 1900 (while retaining its monarchy); Samoa, which remained under Malietoa chieftains until it was annexed by Germany and the US in 1899; Hawaii, whose ruling monarchy was overthrown by American and European residents in 1893, before being annexed by the United States in 1898; and Fiji, which became a British colony in 1874.

CHAPTER SIX:
A NEW WORLD ORDER
1900 to 1945

MIDDLE EAST AND AFRICA

RESISTANCE TO EUROPEAN COLONIAL RULE

As Europeans rushed to lay claim to the African continent, subjugated Africans rose up in rebellion against their oppressors. Resistance, however, lacked cohesion and the superior military technology of the Europeans crushed most opposition movements.

North-east Africa, in the present-day states of Egypt, Sudan and Somalia, saw some of the most tenacious resistance, particularly by those who fought in defence of Islam. When Greater Somalia was partitioned between Britain, Italy and Ethiopia during the 'Scramble for Africa', Muslims from across the Horn of Africa formed an army (known as the Dervishes) and carved out a state led by the Somali religious leader Muhammad Abdullah Hassan. The Dervishes held the British at bay for twenty-five years, until aerial bombardment in 1920 finally led to their defeat.

In German South-West Africa (now central Namibia), the Herero people, who had been dispossessed of their land and livestock, staged an uprising between 1904 and 1907. Rebels were shot by the German army or sent to labour camps, with the result that over 75 per cent of the Herero population died (from 80,000 before 1904 to 15,000 in 1911).

Occupation of German East Africa (now Tanzania) also led to violent African resistance, in particular to the German policy of growing cotton for export. The uprising became known as the Maji Maji Rebellion after the Swahili word for water (as a spirit medium had convinced the rebels that his magic water would protect them from German bullets). The German government crushed the rebellion and systematically destroyed villages, crops and food stores. The resulting famine led to over 200,000 deaths.

The Union of South Africa and the Ethiopian Empire

In 1910, the former Dutch colonies of Transvaal and Orange Free State united with the Cape Colony and Natal to form the Union of South Africa, a self-governing dominion of the British crown.

New laws systematized anti-black legislation in much of the social and economic life of South Africa and awarded 90 per cent of the land to the white minority, while the black majority received 10 per cent as 'Native Reserves'. Non-whites were denied the vote in the former colonies of the Transvaal and Orange Free State while the great majority of the black population were disenfranchised in the Cape and Natal.

In response to this systematic discrimination, middle-class black Africans founded in 1912 the South African Native National Congress to advocate for political rights. It was renamed the African National Congress in 1923 and become more of an active mass movement from the mid-1940s onwards.

Ethiopia had secured the distinction of being almost the only African nation to have resisted colonization after its defeat of an Italian invasion in 1896. In 1917, Prince Ras Tafari took power, becoming emperor in 1930 as Haile Selassie ('Power of the Holy Trinity'). He worked to modernize the country and between 1936 and 1941 lived in exile in Britain during the Italian occupation of Ethiopia. After British forces had liberated Ethiopia, Selassie returned and in 1942 outlawed slavery (in the 1930s, there were an estimated 2 million slaves out of a population of 26 million). The Rastafari movement, begun in Jamaica in the 1930s, reveres Haile Selassie as a messianic figure who would lead the people of Africa to freedom. Many of its followers, known as Rastafarians, are still found in Jamaica and across the world.

THE DISSOLUTION OF THE OTTOMAN EMPIRE

The Ottoman Empire had long been known as the 'sick man of Europe', having lost in the nineteenth century many of its European territories (namely Greece, Serbia, Montenegro and Romania) and Arab provinces (Algeria and Tunis to the French, and Egypt to the British).

In 1908, the Austro-Hungarian Empire annexed the former Ottoman territories of Bosnia and Hercegovina and in the same year Bulgaria declared its independence. During the Italo–Turkish War (1911–12), in which the Ottomans lost modern-day Libya, the Balkan League (made up of Montenegro, Bulgaria, Greece and Serbia) attacked Turkey. The ensuing Balkan Wars (1912–13) led to defeat for the Ottomans and the loss of virtually all of its Balkan possessions.

The defeat of the Ottoman Empire in the First World War finally led to its complete dissolution, forcing it to give up all its non-Turkish territories in the Treaty of Sèvres (1920). Syria, after a brief period of independence, became a French mandate (in other words, commissioned by the League of Nations to administer a territory), while Palestine, Jordan and Iraq became British mandates.

In 1923, following the departure of Sultan Mehmet VI, the Republic of Turkey was proclaimed, with the army general Mustafa Kemal as its first president. Given the name 'Atatürk' (meaning 'Father of the Turks'), he introduced many political and social reforms – including abolishing the caliphate, introducing new civil and criminal law codes, adopting the Latin alphabet, and giving women the vote – all designed to make Turkey a modern, secular state.

PALESTINE AND THE ZIONIST MOVEMENT

Formerly part of the Ottoman Empire, Palestine (the official political title given to the land west of the River Jordan, including the holy places of Jerusalem and Nazareth) was granted to Britain as a mandate following the First World War.

Included in the mandate was the Balfour Declaration (1917) in which the British government formally declared its support of the Zionist movement (see below) favouring the establishment of a national home for Jewish people in Palestine. The Arab Palestinians rejected the mandate and there followed periods of unrest and rioting as Jews and Arabs clashed. In response, the Jews set up their own military organization, Haganah, which aimed to defend Jewish settlements from Arab attack.

Jewish settlement in Palestine developed slowly until Nazi persecution of German Jews in the 1930s led to increased immigration. This alarmed the Arab population who between 1936 and 1939 revolted and attacked Jewish settlers. The Zionist movement (named after Mount Zion, which had been the site of the fortress of Jerusalem), which had grown in force since the World Zionist Conference of 1897, thereafter split when a right-wing extremist group, the Stern Gang, targeted the British presence in Palestine.

During the Arab revolt, the British government, concluding that the two sides could not be reconciled, suggested dividing Palestine into Jewish and Arab states. The proposal was rejected, after which the Second World War intervened, which led to a vast increase in illegal Jewish immigration and renewed terrorism in Palestine. The eventual formation of the state of Israel by the United Nations in 1948 marked the success of the Zionist movement.

FAR EAST

The Boxer Rebellion and the Chinese Revolution of 1911

The Qing (Manchu) dynasty in China never fully recovered from the Taiping Rebellion (1853–64 – see page 121), and over subsequent years faced increasing intervention from European powers keen to extend their commercial activities throughout the country.

This foreign intrusion, combined with increasing Christian missionary activity, caused deep resentment and led to a popular movement by members of a secret organization, The Society of Righteous and Harmonious Fists, known as the Boxer Rebellion (1898–1901). Beginning in the north of China, where the import of foreign goods had caused severe unemployment, the Boxers killed or attacked foreign missionaries, Chinese Christians and foreign embassies, and destroyed railway and telegraph lines.

After foreigners were forced to seek refuge in the Legation Quarter of Beijing (and the German ambassador was killed), European powers sent in an allied force of 20,000 troops in August 1900. In September 1901 the Empress Dowager Cixi was forced to accept the harsh terms of the Peace Protocol, which gave foreigners even greater control of Chinese revenue. Russia took the opportunity to seize Manchuria (leading to the Russo–Japanese War of 1904–5) and the British invaded Tibet, although China was not subject to partition by European powers partly because the fanaticism of the Boxers showed that any such attempt would lead to massive popular resistance.

The Qing dynasty, however, was irretrievably weakened and would eventually be swept away in the Chinese Revolution of 1911. Revolutionaries, led by Sun Yat-sen, had formed the anti-Manchu Revolutionary Alliance in 1905, and had begun to spread revolutionary propaganda. After the Wuchang Uprising in October 1911, provincial delegates declared a republic with Sun Yat-sen as the provisional president of the Kuomintang (or Nationalist Party). In February 1912 the last Qing emperor Puyi, aged just six, was forced to abdicate, thus ending 2,000 years of imperial rule in China.

THE RISE OF JAPAN

By 1900, Japan had transformed itself into an industrialized world power, with a modern army and a navy that by 1920 was the third largest in the world. This new strength had led to victories against China (First Sino–Japanese War, 1894–5) and Russia (Russo–Japanese War, 1904–5), and the occupation of Taiwan (1895) and Korea (1910).

Thereon, Japan increasingly followed expansionary and militaristic policies, aimed largely at dominating China and the Far East, thereby securing access to raw materials and markets that were vital to the economic development of Japan, a resource-poor nation. The First World War, in which Japan fought on the side of the Allies, enabled Japan to widen its territorial holdings (seizing Germany's territories in the northern islands of the Pacific). Japan also wielded huge influence in Manchuria in north-east China, in order to control its coal and iron ore deposits. In 1931, Japanese troops seized the Manchurian capital of Mukden, overran the province and in 1932 set up the puppet state of Manchukuo (with Emperor Puyi installed as the figurehead sovereign).

In 1937, Japan invaded other parts of China, precipitating the Second Sino–Japanese War (1937–45). By the end of 1938, the Japanese had overrun northern China, capturing Shanghai, Nanjing, Guanghzhou and Hankou. In the 'Rape of Nanjing', over 100,000 civilians were massacred by Japanese troops. By 1939 the war had reached stalemate, with Japanese forces unable to defeat Communist troops in Shaanxi. In 1940, Japan invaded French Indochina, and in 1941 attacked the US naval base at Pearl Harbor, thus entering the Second World War. Following the atomic bombings of Hiroshima and Nagasaki and Japan's unconditional surrender in 1945 (see pages 171–3), Japanese forces withdrew from China, its empire largely eliminated by the Allies who restored the independence of its former colonies.

THE CHINESE CIVIL WAR

Following the Chinese Revolution of 1911, the Kuomintang (or Nationalist Party) proved ineffective as a central power as local warlords reassumed control over their respective territories. In the late 1920s, the Kuomintang managed to reunify the country through a military campaign known as the 'Northern Expedition', moving the capital from Beijing to Nanjing.

At the same time, the Chinese Communist Party, founded in 1921 in Shanghai and purged by the Kuomintang in 1927, had retreated to the countryside, combined with peasant rebels and established control over several areas in southern China. In 1931, the Marxist revolutionary leaders Mao Zedong and Zhu De created a Chinese Communist republic in Jiangxi (Jiangxi Soviet) and saw it expand to cover an area with a population of 9 million. They resisted several attempts by the Kuomintang to remove them, until they were finally forced in 1934 to move out of the province. Under the leadership of Mao, an army of 80,000 fought its way north on a year-long journey – famously known as the Long March – from Jiangxi to Shaanxi province. Around 20,000 survived the journey, including Mao who set up the communist headquarters at Ya-An, and continued to resist the Kuomintang.

In 1937, the Communists and Nationalists agreed to join together to fight the Japanese in the Second Sino–Japanese War. The Communists proved an effective resistance force against the Japanese, and continued to extend their influence so that by the end of the war around 96 million people in China were under Communist control. The resumption of civil war between the Kuomintang and Chinese Communist Party in 1946 led to a crushing victory for the Communists, and in 1949 the People's Democratic Republic of China was proclaimed with Mao as its first head of state.

TOWARDS INDIA'S INDEPENDENCE

British rule in India came under increasing pressure from nationalists seeking independence. The Indian National Congress, founded in 1885 initially to further Indian participation in government, was led from 1920 by the Hindu spiritual leader Mohandas Gandhi. Known as Mahatma (meaning 'great soul'), Gandhi's aim was to achieve self-rule in India by non-violent means. In 1916 the Congress had also joined forces with the Muslim League to promote Hindu–Muslim unity.

During the First World War, Indian troops had served the British loyally but nationalist agitation in India had increased, causing the British raj to introduce anti-terrorist laws. In response, Gandhi urged his followers to stop work, and a large strike was planned in Amritsar in April 1919. Government forces arrested the strike's ring-leaders, then fired on a large crowd that had gathered, killing 372 and wounding over 1,200. This led to violent rioting throughout the Punjab and mounting agitation in India.

Thereon the Congress Party gained mass support, as hundreds of thousands joined Gandhi's civil-disobedience campaigns and boycotted British-made products and institutions. The government responded by arresting Gandhi and 60,000 others in 1930 and by 1931 had largely gained control of the country, although civil disobedience continued. By 1937, the Congress had secured considerable success in provincial elections, although it rejected the British offer of dominion status and continued its call for outright independence.

By 1947, amid clashes between Hindus and Muslims, the Congress Party and the Muslim League agreed to the partitioning of the subcontinent into the self-ruling dominions of India and Pakistan. Gandhi, however, was opposed to partition and stayed away from celebrations in Delhi, only to be murdered by a Hindu fanatic when he returned to the city.

EUROPE

THE TRIPLE ENTENTE AND THE ARMS RACE

By 1900, heightened tensions between the Great Powers of Europe led to the establishment of various intricate alliances. These were meant to create stability in Europe, but the complex network of treaties and guarantees would ultimately drag all of the European Great Powers into multinational war.

After the Franco–Prussian War, Otto von Bismarck, Chancellor of the newly united German Empire, sought to isolate France by forming a triple alliance with Italy and Austria in 1882. Thereafter, Germany grew in military and industrial might, and in 1898 began an ambitious naval building programme designed to challenge the maritime supremacy of Great Britain.

In 1904, France and Great Britain, both of whom had become increasingly isolated in the latter half of the nineteenth century, formalized a 'friendly agreement' known as the Entente Cordiale. It in effect ensured that the two nations would not interfere in each other's colonial interests abroad. In 1894, France had also formed a dual alliance with Russia, to create a strong counter to Germany's Triple Alliance. In 1907, Great Britain signed the Anglo-Russian Entente. Together the three powers now became the Triple Entente.

A fierce arms race between Britain and Germany (sparked in part by the launch of Great Britain's powerful new class of battleship, typified by HMS *Dreadnought*, in 1906) extended to the rest of Europe, as all the major powers modernized and escalated their spending on armed forces and weaponry in readiness for war.

THE OUTBREAK OF THE FIRST WORLD WAR AND THE WESTERN FRONT

The trigger for war came on 28 June 1914 in the Bosnian capital, Sarajevo, when a teenage Bosnian Serb assassinated the Archduke Franz Ferdinand, heir to the Austrian throne. Austria-Hungary, threatened by Serbia's territorial gains during the Balkan Wars, declared war on Serbia on 28 July. A week later, through various complex alliances, all of the great European powers were drawn into the conflict: Russia, in support of Serbia, mobilized its forces along the Austrian and German borders; Germany then declared war on Russia and its ally France, and, implementing its plan for a pre-emptive attack on France, invaded Belgium on 3 August; Britain, honouring its promise to protect Belgium's neutrality, declared war on Germany on 4 August.

The conflict soon drew in other nations and rivalries: Japan joined in on the side of the Allies (France, Great Britain and Russia) as, later, did Italy, Portugal, Romania and eventually the USA and Greece; while the Ottoman Empire and Bulgaria allied themselves with the Central Powers (Germany and Austria-Hungary).

Having pushed back British forces in Belgium, Germany swept into north-west France, intending to knock out France in six weeks. Her advance, however, was thrown back at the Battle of Marne and the German advance to the Channel Ports was stopped at the First Battle of Ypres.

Thereafter both sides settled down to trench warfare, having dug hundreds of miles of defensive trenches from the border of Switzerland to the Belgian coast. Key battles between 1914 and 1917 were fought at Ypres, with the third (the Battle of Passchendaele, July to November 1917) resulting in over half a million casualties. At Verdun, the Germans tried to bleed the French Army to death in 1916 but the French forced them back. At the same time, further north on the Somme, another struggle led to one of the bloodiest battles ever recorded, with over 1 million casualties (including 57,470 British casualties – more than 19,000 of them killed – on the first day of battle alone).

Three years of bitter trench warfare, marked by unprecedented levels of casualties (caused by a variety of modern weaponry, mainly artillery, but also trench mortars, machine guns and hand grenades), led only to stalemate, with the line moving no more than 10 miles (16 km) either way.

THE EASTERN FRONT AND OTHER THEATRES OF WAR

The inability to break through the deadlock on the battlefield caused the war to move to new fronts. In Eastern Europe, the Russians had invaded East Prussia in 1914 but were defeated at the Battle of Tannenberg. They had better luck holding the Austrian province of Galicia before they were pushed back by Austro-Hungarian and German armies, losing Poland to the Germans in August 1915. (By 1918, post-Revolutionary Russia had withdrawn from the conflict following the Treaty of Brest-Litovsk with Germany. Inevitably, this freed large numbers of German and Austro-Hungarian troops, as well as weapons and equipment, that could now be deployed in the West.)

Between April 1915 and January 1916, the Allies (made

up of British, French, Australian and New Zealand troops) tried to force the Ottoman Turks out of the war through the Gallipoli Campaign in Turkey, but were forced to retreat. They had more success in the Middle East, eventually breaking through the Ottoman line in Gaza in 1917 and occupying Jerusalem, aided by an Arab revolt (in which T. E. Lawrence 'of Arabia' and other British officers were involved). In 1918 Allied troops defeated the Turks at Megiddo in Syria and occupied Damascus. A second campaign in Mesopotamia led to the conquest of much of what is now Iraq and the capture of Baghdad in March 1917, although not before a large British and Indian Army force had been defeated and captured at Kut al-Amara.

In Africa, Britain's Commonwealth allies and France targeted Germany's colonies, taking Togoland in 1914 and Cameroon in 1916. South Africa conquered South-West Africa in 1915, although a German guerrilla campaign prevented the same success in East Africa. In the Pacific, German colonies fell to Japanese, Australian and New Zealand troops. In north-east Italy, a long and disastrous campaign after Italy had joined the Allies in 1915 finally led to victory against Austria-Hungary in 1918, though not before the Italian Army had been reinforced with British and French (and some American) troops from the Western Front following the disastrous Italian defeat at Caporetto late in 1917.

At sea, despite the frenzied naval arms race before the war (see page 155), the only major sea battle between British and German fleets fought in 1916 at Jutland (Denmark) was inconclusive; however, the German High Seas fleet did not put to sea again in force thereafter. Germany's unrestricted

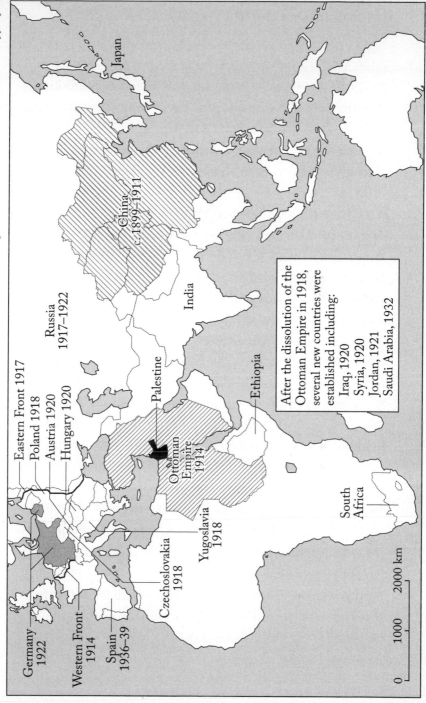

After the dissolution of the Ottoman Empire in 1918, several new countries were established including:

Iraq, 1920
Syria, 1920
Jordan, 1921
Saudi Arabia, 1932

submarine warfare, a policy implemented in February 1915, had more success as it cut off supply lines to Britain, although the sinking of the *Lusitania* passenger liner in April that year, with the loss of many American lives at a time when their country was still neutral, contributed to the United States's crucial decision to enter the war on the Allied side in 1917.

The End of the Great War

A massive German offensive, aimed at victory before American troops arrived in strength, combined with Britain's tightly controlled naval blockade of Germany (which had seriously depleted Germany's stock of raw materials and foodstuffs) led to an abrupt end to hostilities. The Germans launched their assault in March 1918, using troops transferred from the Eastern Front, after fighting had ceased in Russia in February 1918. German troops on the Western Front now numbered 3.5 million. The Allies, however, with the help of newly arrived American forces, held their line and counter-attacked, finally piercing the previously impregnable 'Hindenburg Line' at the end of September 1918. The worn-out German Army was forced to retreat and the armistice, bringing an end to hostilities on the Western Front, was signed on 11 November. By then, Bulgaria, Austria-Hungary and Turkey had already concluded armistices with the Allies.

The war proved to be one of the deadliest conflicts in history, with 30 million civilian and military casualties (approximately 8.5 million war dead). From 1919–23 delegates dominated by the US, Britain and France negotiated a number of peace treaties, often known as the Paris Peace Settlement. The Treaty of Versailles held Germany responsible for the outbreak of the war, forcing it to pay reparations to the Allies for damages caused in the war and strictly limiting its armed forces. German colonial possessions were given up, along with European territories, such as Alsace-Lorraine to France and west Prussia to the restored nation of Poland. The League of Nations was also set up as an intergovernmental peacekeeping organization backed by the Great Powers.

Treaties were also made with Austro-Hungary, Bulgaria and what remained of the Ottoman Empire. Austro-Hungary was effectively dismantled, to form a small Austria, a separate Hungary, a resurrected Poland, an enlarged Serbia called Yugoslavia and an entirely new Czechoslovakia. Bulgaria was forced to cede territory to Romania, Greece and Yugoslavia, and the dissolved Ottoman Empire re-formed into the Republic of Turkey (see page 148), with Syria ceded to a French mandate and Palestine and Jordan to a British administration.

The Spanish Flu

As one of the deadliest conflicts in history drew to a close, an influenza outbreak known as the 1918 flu pandemic (or 'Spanish Flu') emerged, adding another 20 to 40 million deaths to a world already ravaged by war.

It's thought the first wave of the pandemic originated in Camp Funston, Kansas, in the US, in March 1918. In the following month, a huge mobilization of American troops began to arrive in Western Europe, carrying the virus with them. In August 1918 the disease had mutated into a more lethal version, with a third deadly wave occurring in the following winter. Once contracted the virus spread quickly, killing up to 20 per cent of those infected, often just two days after the first indication of symptoms. Unusually for influenza, most of its victims were healthy adults between the ages of twenty and forty, whose stronger immune systems adversely enabled the virus to ravage their bodies.

The pandemic affected almost every part of the inhabited world, killing approximately 3 per cent of the world's population, making it one of the deadliest natural disasters in human history. In India around 10–17 million people died, in Indonesia 1.5 million people died (out of a population of 30 million). In the US about 675,000 lost their lives to the virus, in Britain over 200,000.

By the spring of 1919 the virus had largely run its course: other outbreaks occurred in the 1920s but mortality rates were far lower.

WOMEN'S SUFFRAGE

Throughout the nineteenth century, women had campaigned for the right to vote. New Zealand was the first country in the world to extend the suffrage to women in 1893, followed by Australia in 1902. In the US, the state of Wyoming gave women over 21 the vote in 1869, although it was 1920 before women across the US attained voting rights. In Europe, the first country to grant women suffrage was Finland in 1906, followed by Norway in 1913, and Russia (as a result of the Revolution) in 1917.

In Britain, the National Union of Women's Suffrage

Societies, known as the 'Suffragists', had been lobbying for universal suffrage since 1897. In 1903, Emmeline Pankhurst set up the more militant Women's Social and Political Union (the 'Suffragettes'). Under the rally cry 'Deeds not Words', they waged a much-publicized campaign that included arson attacks on public buildings and refusing food when imprisoned. On 4 June 1913, the Suffragette Emily Davison famously stepped in front of King George V's horse, Anmer, at the Epsom Derby, and was trampled, dying from her injuries four days later.

During the First World War, both campaigns all but halted their political activities although women, as a result of male conscription, were involved in a variety of jobs traditionally seen as the preserve of men. In 1918, property-owning women over the age of thirty were finally awarded the vote in Britain and by 1928 could vote on equal terms with men.

Elsewhere in Europe, women gained the vote in Germany, Austria and Poland after the war, whereas France didn't grant female suffrage until 1944, Belgium in 1948. The last European country to grant equal voting rights for women was Switzerland in 1971.

THE RUSSIAN REVOLUTIONS AND THE RISE OF THE SOVIET UNION

At the beginning of the twentieth century, heavy taxation had brought mounting distress to Russia's poor, and crushing defeat in the Russo-Japanese War (1904–5) had further aggravated discontent.

Political and social unrest and in particular the firing

on of peaceful demonstrators by government troops in St Petersburg culminated in the Revolution of 1905. Strikes and mutinies within the armed forces forced Tsar Nicholas II to establish a parliament (the State Duma) in 1906. The tsar resisted attempts, however, to move from absolute to constitutional monarchy and social disorder continued as Russia entered the First World War.

In March 1917, a war-torn Russia faced new disturbances in St Petersburg, which culminated in the tsar's abdication (ending over 300 years of imperialist Romanov rule) and the formation of the Provisional Government. In November 1917, during the October Revolution, Vladimir Lenin's Bolshevik party, which had been pushing for socialist revolution, seized power. In the following March, the Bolsheviks signed the Treaty of Brest-Livovsk, marking Russia's exit from the war.

Civil war ensued between the Reds (Bolsheviks) and the Whites (the more conservative anti-Bolshevik Russians, who were supported for a time by Alllied forces). The Russian Communist Party, as the Bolsheviks called themselves from 1918, gained supremacy and established in 1922 the Soviet Union (the union of Russian, Ukrainian, Byelorussian and Transcaucasian Soviet republics). Nicholas II and his family were shot by the Bolsheviks in 1918.

After Lenin's death in 1924, Joseph Vissarionovich Jugashvili, otherwise known as Stalin ('man of steel'), succeeded in 1927 as the Communist Party's uncontested leader. In the following year he launched programmes to expand and collectivize farming and rapidly develop industry. Millions across the Soviet Union died from starvation, including 10 million deaths in Ukraine caused by the 'Great Famine' of 1932–3. In the Great Purges of 1935–8 Stalin eliminated opposition by executing or sending to the Gulag labour camps 'Old Bolsheviks', members of the Intelligentsia, army officers and millions of others. Through these brutal means, the state grew more powerful and industry and agricultural output increased rapidly until the Soviet Union was again devastated by world war – though this time on the winning side.

Mussolini and the Rise of Italian Fascism

In 1919, former primary school teacher and ex-serviceman Benito Mussolini, who before the war had been an extreme socialist, formed a movement called the *fascio di combattimento* ('union for force'). An anti-socialist, anti-capitalist movement, the Fascists (as they came to be called) sought power by any means, including violence aimed at elected authorities and their political enemies. In 1922 Mussolini orchestrated the Blackshirts' March on Rome and was created prime minister, assuming the title 'Il Duce' (the leader) in 1925.

Mussolini organized his government on dictatorial lines, and launched a series of largely unsuccessful government initiatives (such as the 'Battle for Land') designed to combat Italy's economic setbacks and unemployment. Extensive propaganda, through press, radio and schooling, ran alongside many of these schemes in a bid to promote the illusion of Fascist efficiency over that of liberalism and democracy.

Colonization overseas, the creation of 'vital space' for Italian settlers, was also key to Mussolini's Fascist ideology

(Italy, it was claimed, was heir to the Roman Empire and its territorial legacy) – ideas that would spread to Europe and inspire both Hitler in Germany and General Franco in Spain. Mussolini pursued an aggressive foreign policy both in Ethiopia, which he invaded and occupied in 1935, and as a German ally in the Second World War. British troops eventually evicted the Italians from Ethiopia in 1941 (as well as Eritrea and Somalia), and after the Allied invasion of Sicily in 1943, Mussolini was forced to resign. He was rescued from imprisonment by German paratroopers but in 1945 was captured and shot by Italian Communist partisans.

HITLER AND NAZI GERMANY

In 1920–1, an Austrian-born ex-First World War corporal named Adolf Hitler became leader of the National Socialist German Workers' Party (Nazionalsozialistiche Deutsche Arbeiterpartei – or Nazi Party for short). Hitler's talents as an orator drew in support as he called for abandonment of the humiliating terms of the Treaty of Versailles and the expansion of German territory. Hitler also based his Nazi ideology on anti-Semitism and the belief that an Aryan 'master race' existed.

Inspired by the Fascists' rise to power in Italy (1922), Hitler attempted a coup in Munich in 1923 (known as the Beer Hall Putsch), after which he was imprisoned until 1924. During this time he wrote his semi-autobiographical political manifesto *Mein Kampf* (*My Struggle*). The Nazi party continued to expand beyond its Bavarian base and, by promising jobs and national pride, received a huge boost during the recession and high unemployment that followed the Wall Street Crash.

In 1933, Hitler, now Chancellor, established a one-party dictatorship by eliminating his rivals in the 'Night of the Long Knives'. Following the death of the German President Paul von Hindenburg in 1934, Hitler appointed himself Führer (leader) of the German Reich (state). Having already banned other political parties, he developed an invasive police network and assumed total control of the country. The persecution of Jews also began in earnest: the Nuremberg Laws of 1935 deprived Jews of citizenship, Jewish businesses were then confiscated, and in 1938 synagogues were burnt down and Jewish shops looted (an event known as Kristallnacht).

In 1936, Hitler took his first defiant steps by reoccupying the Rhineland (something expressly forbidden by the Treaty of Versailles) and in the same year joined Mussolini in an alliance known as the Rome-Berlin Axis. Britain and France's policy of non-intervention (appeasement) enabled Hitler to annex Austria in 1938, and begin the piecemeal occupation of Czechoslovakia, all of which directly flouted the terms of the Paris treaties.

THE SPANISH CIVIL WAR

Between the end of the First World War and 1936, Spain was seriously divided between political parties and groups keen to overthrow the government. In 1931, Spanish Republicans forced King Alfonso XIII into exile and a new republican government succeeded, which, over the next five years, faced continued riots, protests and revolts.

In 1936, military leaders and other conservatives staged an unsuccessful military coup against the newly elected left-wing Popular Front government, culminating in three years of civil war. General Franco took control of the rebels (the Nationalists) and won the support of Italy's Fascist regime (which sent troops, weapons and equipment) and Nazi Germany (which sent aircraft and aircrew, as well as tanks, artillery, instructors and military advisers). The Republican government was aided by the Soviet Union as well as some 40,000 liberal-minded foreign volunteers from Europe and the US, many of whom viewed the war as a fight against authoritarianism.

The intervention of Fascist Italy and Nazi Germany, however, swayed the balance and the Nationalists steadily won territory in the north and south. In 1938, the Nationalists had split the Republican forces into two and on 5 March 1939 the government was forced into exile. In the following month General Franco established a Fascist dictatorship that lasted to his death in 1975. The war had been marked by almost three years of bloody fighting, resulting in around 1 million deaths (600,000 in battle), a death tally that exceeded the more prolonged American Civil War.

THE SECOND WORLD WAR

On 1 September 1939, Hitler's tanks rolled into west Poland, while later that month Soviet Russian forces invaded from the east. Columns of fast-moving tanks, followed by mobilized infantry and waves of powerful air cover (tactics known as

Blitzkrieg: 'Lightning War') enabled Germany to overrun the country by 27 September. Two days after the invasion, Britain and France had abandoned their policies of appeasement and declared war on Germany.

The Soviet Union thereon occupied the Baltic States and attacked Finland. Germany, after a lull of six months, invaded and conquered Denmark and Norway in April 1940, then advanced into Holland, Belgium and France. German panzer (armoured) divisions, in their dash towards France's Channel coast, cut off the British Expeditionary Force from French forces further south. British Prime Minister Winston Churchill ordered an evacuation from Dunkirk and between 26 May and 4 June some 338,000 British and French troops were ferried back to the UK. Just over two weeks later, France had fallen and was occupied by German troops and the Vichy collaborative government under Marshal Pétain, formerly the hero of the French defence of Verdun in 1916.

After the fall of France, Hitler launched a bombing offensive against Britain, although its planned invasion of the country was postponed after it met significant resistance from the Royal Air Force during the Battle of Britain (July to October 1940). Nonetheless, sustained bombing of British cities, known as the Blitz, continued between September 1940 and May 1941, killing around 40,000 civilians.

Pro-Nazi governments of Romania, Bulgaria and Slovakia joined the Axis Powers, and Hitler conquered Yugoslavia and Greece before invading Russia in June 1941. After huge territorial gains, the main German advance was barred by the Soviet defence of Stalingrad. The Germans reached the centre but a massive Soviet counter-attack trapped them in the city, and the German commander-in-chief surrendered in January 1943. With up to 2 million military and civilian casualties on both sides, the defeat marked the end of Germany's advance into Russia and a major turning point in the war.

THE CONCLUSION OF THE SECOND WORLD WAR

Another critical point in the war occurred in late 1942 at El Alamein on the Egyptian coast, some 150 miles north-west of Cairo. General Montgomery's British and Allied forces secured a decisive victory over German and Italian forces under Rommel, preventing them from occupying Egypt and advancing towards the Suez Canal. A month later Anglo-American forces landed in Morocco and Algeria and by May 1943, following the surrender of all Axis forces in Tunisia, controlled the whole of the North African coast.

Meanwhile at sea, German U-boats in the Battle of the Atlantic had been attacking Allied merchant shipping, claiming an average of 96 ships per month in 1942. By 1943, however, better radar and intelligence gleaned through the British decryption of the German cipher machine, Enigma, enabled Britain to re-route convoys away from U-boat 'wolf packs'. Enigma intelligence, codenamed 'Ultra' by the British, was also crucial in Allied victories in North Africa, Italy and Normandy.

The US, which had joined the war on the side of the Allies after Japan had bombed Pearl Harbor in 1941, was also aided by decrypted enemy communications, enabling American naval forces to ambush and defeat the Japanese fleet at the

Battle of the Coral Sea in May 1942 and the Battle of the Midway in the following month. By 1943, the US had effective air and sea dominance in the Pacific and recaptured several occupied Japanese territories. In 1944 US and British land campaigns had also recovered the Philippines and Burma.

In Europe, American and British strategic bombings of German towns, cities, military zones and factories between May 1942 and May 1945, caused devastation, particularly in Hamburg, Dresden and Berlin, resulting in 750,000 to 1 million civilian deaths.

In July 1943, Allied troops conquered Sicily, Mussolini was overthrown, and an invasion of the Italian mainland began in September. After nine months of fierce German resistance, the Allies reached Rome.

The Allied invasion of France began on 6 June 1944 (D-Day), when 150,000 men landed on five Normandy beaches, broke through the German defences and eventually liberated Paris on 25 August. Thereafter the Allies pushed through Europe, suffering heavy casualties in the Ardennes at the Battle of the Bulge. In March 1945, the Allies entered Germany and linked up with the Soviet Army. Hitler committed suicide on 30 April, and on 8 May 1945 the Allies accepted Germany's unconditional surrender and declared Victory in Europe (VE-Day).

VICTORY IN JAPAN AND THE HOLOCAUST

Three months after VE-Day, on 6 and 9 August 1945, the US bombers dropped atomic bombs on the Japanese cities of Hiroshima and Nagasaki. Some 175,000 Japanese civilians

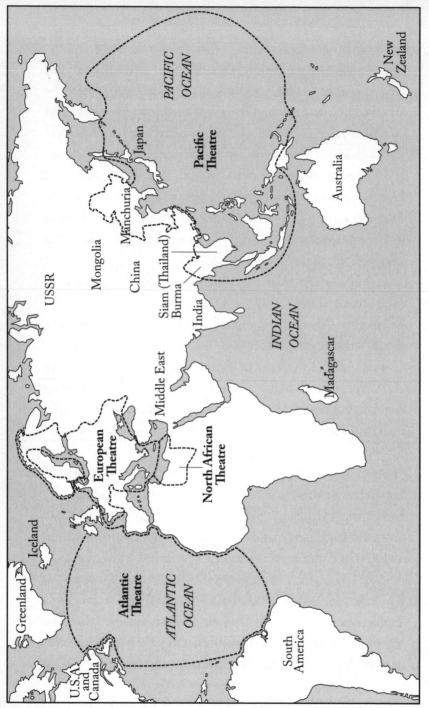

7 Main Theatres of the Second World War

died immediately but many others later perished or suffered from radiation poisoning and burns. This, combined with the Soviet Union's declaration of war on Japan on 14 August, forced Japan to surrender.

Following the German surrender, leaders from the key Allied nations – Stalin, Truman (who had succeeded Roosevelt as US president on the latter's death in April 1945) and Churchill (and later Attlee, following Churchill's and the Conservatives' defeat in the general election), met at the Potsdam Conference in July and August 1945. They agreed on the terms of Germany's reparation and its division into four Allied occupation zones.

In the same year, the United Nations was established to replace the ineffective League of Nations. Its aim was to ensure peace, security and cooperation among the nations of the world and at the Yalta conference it was agreed that membership would be open to nations that had joined the Allies by March 1945. In June 1946, fifty member nations signed the United Nations charter.

Over 50 million lives had been lost during the war, and many of the dead – at least 35 million – were civilians (of whom 20 million were from the Soviet Union and 4.5 million from Poland). At least 10 million, and perhaps as many as 17 million, civilians were deliberately exterminated as a result of Nazi ideological policies, including the systematic genocide of some 6 million Jews during the Holocaust. Jewish people in Nazi-occupied lands were moved into ghettos (60,000 died of starvation or deprivation in the Warsaw Ghetto in 1940) or forced-labour camps. Many (Jewish and non-Jewish) civilians were also killed in mass-shootings, a practice that escalated to horrific proportions as the Nazis advanced into Eastern Europe and western Russia during 1941 and 1942.

The 'final solution' for the Jewish 'problem', as agreed by leading Nazis in early 1942, came in the form of death camps, six of which were built in Poland in 1942. Here, another 1.5 million Jews were killed, along with Soviet and Polish POWs, political opponents, the disabled or mentally ill, homosexuals and other minority groups transported from across Nazi-occupied Europe.

THE AMERICAS

THE ROARING TWENTIES, THE GREAT DEPRESSION AND ROOSEVELT'S NEW DEAL

The Roaring Twenties marked a period of economic boom and cultural vibrancy felt throughout many of America's cities in the 1920s.

Mass production fed increasing consumer demand as household appliances came into general use and electrical consumption doubled. The automobile industry – spearheaded by the US car manufacturer Henry Ford – saw huge growth, so that by 1930, one in five Americans owned a car (a figure that Britain wouldn't reach until the 1960s). The advances in the airline and construction industries, the emergence of radio and motion pictures, the rise in popularity of jazz music and dancing all fed into a general mood of modernity.

This era of prosperity ended abruptly with the Wall Street Crash of 1929, which signalled the beginning of the Great

Depression. US banks were forced to call in their European loans and raise tariffs, and countries around the world were hit hard as international trade plummeted. In the US, the fall in crop prices led to deprivation in rural areas, hundreds of thousands of people found themselves homeless, and around 14 million were left unemployed. As industry declined, there was also fall in the demand for raw materials, which affected Africa, the Far East and South America.

By 1933, one fifth of the banks that had existed in 1930 had closed and unemployment had reached 23.6 per cent. That year the new president, Franklin D. Roosevelt, promised to confront the Depression with a series of economic reforms known as the 'New Deal'. Reforms included constructing thousands of roads, schools and other public buildings, and in 1935 introducing social security and a job programme for the unemployed. The US economy temporarily improved, although in autumn 1937 the economy took another sharp downturn and the Depression lingered on until 1941, only lifting in the US when the country entered the Second World War.

LATIN-AMERICAN DEVELOPMENTS

The fifth re-election of the Mexican dictator Porfirio Díaz, who had ruled as president since 1877, sparked the 1910 Mexican Revolution. It evolved into a multi-sided civil war, killing some 2–3 million (out of a 1910 population of around 14 million), and lasting sporadically until 1934. The prolonged struggle led to the creation of the National Revolutionary Party in 1929, which, under a succession of names and leaders, held power until 2000.

In Brazil, the Great Depression of the 1930s (see pages 174–5) led to a serious slump in the price in one its main exports, coffee (in 1900 Brazil supplied 75 per cent of world demand). Deepening food shortages and social unrest led to the seizure of power by Getúlio Vargas in 1930. For the next fifteen years, he ruled as a virtual dictator although he modernized Brazil with fiscal, educational and land reforms, thereby improving conditions for the poor.

Elsewhere in Latin America, a number of regimes grew increasingly resentful of US influence in their countries. Large US-owned companies obtained rights to oil fields in places like Peru and Mexico, exerting influence over land reform and internal affairs. In 1924, a Peruvian exile, Victor Raúl Haya de la Torre, founded in Mexico City the American Popular Revolutionary Alliance (APRA), known as the 'Aprista movement', which aimed to fight US imperialism and unify American Indians.

In 1933, the Peruvian president Luis Sánchez Cerro was assassinated by an Aprista supporter, leading to conflict between the government and APRA that would last for more than fifty years. In Mexico, the president Lázaro Cárdenas took over the properties of the US and British oil wells, despite the severing of diplomatic relations and the boycotting of Mexican goods. During the Second World War, with oil a highly sought-after commodity, Mexico began to export it to Nazi Germany and Fascist Italy.

OCEANIA

The Commonwealth of Australia and the Dominion of New Zealand

On 1 January 1901, Australia's six colonies were federated to form the Commonwealth of Australia. A phase of integration and economic growth began and the federal government began to plan the development of the national capital at Canberra. Each state retained regional administration although federal laws took precedence and the government was still subject to British sovereignty (although over the years Australia's government became increasingly independent). The population stood at 3.4 million people of European ancestry although by 1930 Aborigine numbers had dropped to 67,000 (from 1 million pre-1788) and the government had begun to move many of them to large reserves.

During the First World War, Australia remained a staunchly loyal ally of Britain, joining New Zealand soldiers to form the Anzacs (Australian and New Zealand Army Corps). The country was badly hit by the Depression, with many Australians suffering extreme poverty, although its economy recovered quickly.

In 1907 New Zealand assumed self-governing dominion status within the British Empire (having refused in 1901 to join the new Commonwealth of Australia), and by the 1920s it was largely self-governing.

The Great Depression affected New Zealand's economy severely, and the subsequent social distress led to the election in 1935 of the first Labour government, which introduced a comprehensive welfare state. The new government also argued that Maoris should have equal rights in housing and social benefits. During the Second World War, however, the Maori were exempted from conscription although they volunteered in large numbers (approximately 17,000 took part in the war). In 1947, New Zealand was granted full independence.

SELECT BIBLIOGRAPHY

Ansary, Tamim, *Destiny Disrupted: A History of the World through Islamic Eyes*, PublicAffairs, 2010

Brazier, Chris, *The No-Nonsense Guide to World History*, second revised edition, New Internationalist, 2006

Davies, Norman, *Europe: A History*, new edition, Pimlico, 1997

Encyclopaedia Britannica (online edition: http://www.britannica.com/)

Gombrich, E. H., *A Little History of the World*, Yale University Press, 2008

Grant, Neil, *Oxford Children's History of the World*, new edition, Oxford University Press, 2006

Haywood, John, *The Ancient World: A Complete Guide to History's Great Civilizations from Egypt to the Roman Republic*, Quercus, 2010

Keen, Maurice, *The Pelican History of Medieval Europe*, Penguin, 1969

Kinder, Hermann and Hilgemann, Werner, *The Penguin Atlas of World History*, Volume 1, *From Prehistory to the Eve of the French Revolution*, updated edition, Penguin, 2004; Volume 2, *From the French Revolution to the Present*, Penguin, 2004

Roberts, J. M., *The Hutchinson History of the World*, Helicon, 1992

Somerset Fry, Plantagenet, *History of the World: From the Ancient Egyptians to the Asian Tsunami – the Ultimate Guide to the History of the World*, Dorling Kindersley, 2007

Townson, Duncan (ed.), *The New Penguin Dictionary of Modern History 1789–1945*, Penguin, 1994

Wright, Edmund and Law, Jonathan (eds), *Oxford Dictionary of World History*, second edition, Oxford University Press, 2006

INDEX